The Hampden Railroad

The Greatest Railroad that Never Ran

Philip E. Johnson

i

Second Printing 2014

ISBN: 978-1-304-73390-0

DEDICATION

This book is dedicated to my loving wife, Esther, whose infinite patience made me stick with this project to its completion. Before the internet she spent hours reading and copying microfilm at the Springfield Library obtaining original newspaper articles. She and a girlfriend photographed county railroad maps with a 35mm film camera in the basement of the Hampden County Registry of Deeds one entire day. During the 70's and 80's with children in tow, we walked miles of the abandoned roadbed looking for evidence of the Hampden. In the 90's I began blending our research and Esther began assembling the file for this book. When life caused the book to take a back seat like it did for a few years, Esther would start pushing it to the front and I'd start working on it again. Here it is. It's finally done. Thanks, Esther for all your help.

DISCLAIMER

Nothing in this book should be taken as anything to discredit or defame any individual mentioned. All opinions that are noted are as a result of newspaper reports from the time period, and nothing more.

Most of the images used in this publication are from the Author's, private collection. There are other photographs from several private collections and the internet. In researching the internet I have found copies of photos that have been published on the internet without permission of the original owners. I received permission to use and I have given credit those owners.

CONTENTS

	DEDICATION	vi
1	A LITTLE HISTORY LESSON	Pg 1
2	CONSTRUCTION OF THE HAMPDEN RAILROAD	Pg 5
3	DESIGN AND SPECIFICATIONS OF THE RAILROAD	Pg 19
4	THE LIFE AND WORK ON THE RAILROADS	Pg 31
5	CUTS AND FILLS	Pg 41
6	STATIONS	Pg 57
7	THE BIRCHAM BEND BRIDGE	Pg 61
8	SWIFT RIVER VIADUCT	Pg 71
9	BROAD BROOK	Pg 77
10	OPENING DAY-- THE BEGINNING OF THE END	Pg 83
11	INDUSTRIAL CONNECTION	Pg 99
12	STORIES I'VE BEEN TOLD	Pg 103
13	EPILOGUE/EPITAPH	Pg 105
14	A TRIP ON THE HAMPDEN TODAY-2013	Pg 107
	Appendix A – Hampden Expenses	Pg 109
	Appendix B – Station Numbers	Pg 111
	Appendix C – Obituary of Ralph D. Gillett	Pg 113
	Appendix D – Recreated Spring 1913 Train Schedule	Pg 117
	Index	Pg 119
	Works Cited	Pg 121
	About the Author	Pg 124

ACKNOWLEDGMENTS

I would like to acknowledge the late Robert Buck, who started me on this journey. He gave me a hand sketch of the seven railroads of Palmer, and noting that no one had done a comprehensive book on the Hampden and encouraged me to continue working on it for many years.

My Palmer friends, Phil Opielowski, and Larry Lowenthal, also gave me encouragement and guidance.

The late Lloyd MacNayr, who helped me obtain the construction photo books, some of which are shared in this book.

Mark Austin who helped me with the loan of and obtaining permission for use of the Madeline Bowler collection of the Charles Fuller photos.

CHAPTER ONE

A LITTLE HISTORY LESSON

1910 Western Massachusetts Railroad Scene

East/west railroad travel was dominated by the Boston & Albany and the New Haven shoreline through Boston South Station and Boston & Maine through North Station. North/South travel was dominated by the central Vermont through Connecticut, Massachusetts, and Vermont, the Connecticut River line of the Boston & Maine thru Springfield, Massachusetts where it joined the New Haven Springfield line. There were various branch lines of the New Haven, Boston and Albany, and the Boston & Maine serving small towns almost everywhere in the region. The Boston & Maine Fitchburg line was operating at capacity, while the Boston and Albany was not. More traffic to the Midwest was expected from the ports in the east. Big money in Connecticut and Rhode Island demanded that traffic from Boston to New York City be dominated by the New Haven's shoreline route, even though the inland route by the New York Central to Springfield then via the New Haven was shorter.

However, you could not get from southern areas of New England and New York via Boston to northern areas including Maine without changing stations. One solution was to connect the New Haven Railroad to the Boston & Maine Railroad in Western Massachusetts. This route was shorter than the Boston and Albany mainline, and could allow faster passenger trains.

The route from Boston to Springfield by the Boston & Albany is 98.60 miles, but using the proposed Mass Central & Hampden Railroad route it would be only 97.72 miles.

Also at this time the Southern New England Railroad was being built from Palmer to link the Central Vermont with the port of Providence, Rhode Island. (Another story, told in The Titanic Railroad by Larry Lowenthal)

Late in 1886, October and December, there were newspaper articles discussing the connections of the Central Mass to the Boston and Albany and the New York and New England tracks near Oak Grove Cemetery in Springfield (this was part of the New York, New Haven, & Hartford/Penn Central/Conrail/Boston & Maine-Armory Branch-now abandoned). At this time, the Boston and Albany connected here. This is near the large oil tanks off St James Ave. By the early 1900's, The Boston and Albany had recently re-aligned it's entrance in the Springfield downtown area from the New York and New England main line to its current location. This re-alignment removed the junction and small yard from the area near Oak Grove Cemetery. The Boston and Albany/New Haven had shared the trackage into Springfield from here.

In 1891, the original route of the Central Mass was planned to connect at Springfield, but the powerful Boston and Albany blocked the plans, and the Central Mass changed its route at Bondsville to connect at Northampton.

There has been some confusion of the name Hampden Railroad outside the Railroad community. There was an older railroad with a similar name: The Hampden and Hampshire Railroad that followed the 1840's canal of the same name, which ran from New Haven to Northampton. This is now the Pioneer Valley Railroad north of Westfield, and much of the balance is abandoned New Haven (Penn Central/Conrail) trackage.

Boston & Maine/New Haven Connections

Charles Sanger Mellen became president of the New Haven in 1903 and in 1910 he also became President of the Boston & Maine Railroad, (at this time, the Boston & Maine included the Maine Central). In the 1880's, Mellen was General Manager of the Boston & Maine and purchased land in Palmer for the Central Mass branch line. Mellen had the financial backing of his mentor, JP Morgan, a prominent New York banker.

The New Haven and New York Central railroads had a working relationship. JP Morgan fit Mellen into his plans for control of all the New England Railroads. There were secret meetings on JP Morgan's yacht, the Corsair, one of which produced two significant outcomes:

1. New York Central discontinued exchanges with New Haven competitors, and
2. Both railroads cooperated to gain consent of the New York Central and Mass legislatures.

In 1900, JP Morgan bought the Old Colony, the Boston and Providence, the Providence and Worcester, and the New York and New England Railroads. The Central New England remained independent, but due to Corsair #1, they had no interchange from the Pennsylvania Railroad, New York Central or New Haven, and also couldn't make their interest payments.

The Central New England Railroad completed its interchange near Springfield, MA at a place called Agawam Junction in 1902, but later abandoned this branch in 1921 as traffic decreased.

In 1903, exchanges were arranged with Central New England and Pennsylvania Railroad, Boston and Albany, and Erie Railroads and also the Central New England began to operate at a profit.

In November 1903, Charles Mellen came back to New England from the Northern Pacific Railroad, and in 1904, he orchestrated the New Haven's purchase of 83% of the Central New England Railway. This allowed the New Haven to divert traffic to the Poughkeepsie Bridge, away from the expensive float operation at New York City.

In 1907, Ralph Gillett (pronounced Jill it) had planned a right of way for the Buffalo, Rochester & Eastern Railroad, creating a very nice rail line, with low grades, and gradual curves. The engineering firm of Durkee, White and Towne laid out the line. However, this line was never built.

Holbrook, Cabot, and Rollins constructed the Pittsburg, Binghamton, and Eastern Railroad during 1906--07 to bring coal reserves from Pennsylvania to New York and the New England states. This story is similar to the Hampden's, involving two State Legislatures, other big railroads, and stocks.

In 1911, there was an agreement between JP Morgan and CS Mellen that the New Haven should share the control of the Boston and Albany. This gave the New Haven-Boston & Maine control over almost all of New England's railroads, except for the Central Vermont. Judge Louis Brandies oversaw a court case involving the New

Haven Railroad (Mellen), accusing it of monopolizing rail, trolley and steamship companies in southern New England.

Mellen had recently constructed the New York, Westchester and Boston Railroad (1911-1912). This was a very expensive line at the time.

Mellen and Gillett co-operated on the construction of Hampden Railroad and the Trolley line from Huntington to Lee, Mass. This line is known as the Huckleberry Line by local trolley fans.

The "railroad robber-barons" from the previous century were notorious for obtaining funding from towns along the proposed right of way, setting up their own construction companies, and using shady finances. Stock was printed far beyond the company's ability to pay, a practice illegal now.

The Central New England Railway was completed in Connecticut and New York, and completed the branch to Springfield, Mass via Agawam junction in 1902. The Southern New England was under construction in Massachusetts to connect the Central Vermont to a new port in Providence.

1912 in Perspective

Construction in 1912 was heavy difficult back breaking work. There were few modern conveniences. There was lots of manual labor: "pick and shovel" work paying about $1.75 for a 9.5-hour day. Steam-powered drills were used to drill blasting holes into solid rock. Alfred Nobel's dynamite and nitroglycerin were in common use, having recently been used to complete the Hoosac Tunnel. There were no bulldozers. Although the Howe Company had recently invented a tracked vehicle in 1904, they were not very common. Marian and Bucyrus steam shovels, with up to 80 tons capacity, were in use on Railroad projects and the Panama Canal. The Panama Canal was completed a few years before the Hampden Railroad. Electricity was not very common in rural areas. So there were no electric tools or electric light, allowing daylight operations only.

There were few airplanes so there was no aerial photography. There was no modern building and moving equipment. Most loads, like bridge members, were moved by "jib cranes", which were long poles using block and tackle.

Roads were crude, very few were paved. There were no large trucks, and few automobiles. Railroad equipment was all steam powered, no diesels, and only electric use was in major cities with high-density traffic. Telephones were in business use, but not common in homes. The construction companies built work camps, like tarpaper cities near the major work sites. Trolleys and horseback were the common modes of transportation for working-men

In 1913, the Fox Trot became fashionable. Henry Ford introduced the assembly line into his car factory. Zippers became popular. Vitamin A was discovered. This was an important medical discovery. The Sixteenth Amendment to the Constitution established the Federal Income Tax.

A bushel of large pears cost 95 cents, cooking applies were 50 cents a bushel and horseradish was 10 cents a bottle.

An umbrella cost $1.50, patent leather shoes were $2.89 a pair and men's suits were $9.75 and an overcoat was $4.95.

At first glance these prices seem very reasonable until you consider that workers earned less than $9 each week.

Other Railroad Activity in Teens

A line was constructed by the Boston & Maine north from their Ashuelot Branch at Hinsdale, New Hampshire (Dole Junction) to Brattleboro, Vermont. Holbrook, Cabot and Rollins built this line. Robert W. Nimke shows this line in his book *Connecticut River and Connections Volume 1*. He shares many photos of the construction and includes Holbrook, Cabot, and Rollins construction trains with loco 36, an 0-6-0 with a sloped tender, the very same one used on the Hampden. Nimke also shows Marion shovels and 0-4-0's and gravel cars like the ones used on the Hampden. This branch opened June 21, 1913

Also in 1913, the Long Island Railroad opened Jamaica Station, to transfer passengers from their branches to Penn Station.

The only Massachusetts Railroad new construction in 1913 was the Hampden. The relocation of the Boston & Albany Athol Branch for the Hampden, and the on-going work on the Southern New England were underway.

Charles S Mellen played a very active role in railroads in the late 1800's and early 1900's:

- 1886: General Manager, Boston & Maine Railroad
- President, Northern Pacific Railroad
- 1903: President, New Haven Railroad
- 1910: President, Boston & Maine Railroad
- 1911: mentored Ralph Gillett on this project to create:
  - Hampden Railroad
  - Woronoco Construction Company
  - Hampden Invest Co-Banks, private investors
- 1913: forced to vacate the Presidency of B&M and NH railroads as they were forced to split apart

CHAPTER TWO

CONSTRUCTION OF THE HAMPDEN RAILROAD

The Hampden Railroad Corporation was incorporated in Westfield and maintained its general offices in the D. L. Gillett Block at the corner of Elm and Arnold Street in downtown Westfield today. I photographed this building in 2012. Author's photo

The Key Players in the Hampden Railroad were:

J. P. Morgan   Charles S. Mellen   Ralph D. Gillett

- John Pierpont "J. P." Morgan (b April 17, 1837 in Hartford CT – March 31, 1913 Rome Italy) was an American financier, banker, philanthropist and art collector who dominated corporate finance and industrial consolidation during his time. (Wikipedia)

- Charles S Mellen (b August 16, 1852 Hartford CT – November 17, 1927) was an American railroad man whose career culminated in the presidencies of the Northern Pacific Railway (1897-1903) and the New Haven Railroad. (Wikipedia) He played a very active role in railroads starting in the late 1800's and continuing into the early 1900's. In 1886 he was the General Manager of the Boston & Maine Railroad President, and in 1897 the Northern Pacific Railroad. In 1903 he became the President of the New Haven Railroad and in 1910 also the President of the Boston & Maine Railroad.

- Ralph D. Gillett, Director and President, born in 1865 in Westfield and died on October 14, 1913. He was also the owner and President of the Woronoco Construction Co., President of Hampden Investment Company, and a prominent railroad and trolley builder in Western Mass.

- Oren E. Parks was the general manager, born in 1871 in Westfield, graduated from Massachusetts Institute of Technology in 1893, and served as the Westfield town engineer until 1911.

- Archie D. Robinson, of Westfield, was a Hampden Railroad Director, and the Clerk of the Hampden Railroad Corporation & Woronoco Construction Company.

- Attorney Henry W. Ely of Westfield died in 1933. He was a Hampden Railroad Director and Treasurer of the Woronoco Construction Company, His son, Joseph Ely, became a Governor on Massachusetts

- Edgar L. Gillett, a Hampden Railroad Director of Westfield, (son of Ralph D Gillett). In notarized statements in 1914, he is shown as the Hampden Railroad President.

- Arthur W. Eaton of Pittsfield was a Director of the Hampden Railroad.

- Joseph A. Skinner from Holyoke was a Director and Vice President of the Hampden Railroad. He also served on the Board of Directors of the New Haven Railroad and the Woronoco Construction Company.

- Henry H. Bowman of Springfield was a Director of the Hampden Railroad and the Woronoco Construction Company.

Engineering

Durkee, White and Towne was chosen as the engineering firm. Their offices were located in the Patton Building, 11 Hampden St., Springfield. The principals of the firm were Henry S, Durkee, born in 1863, who graduated from Tufts engineering school in 1888; C T. White, a railroad engineer with 30 years experience, and H. H. Towne, with 25 years experience. Harold Murphy was responsible for the west end and William Johnson was responsible for the east end. Durkee, White and Towne had designed many trolley lines in the previous 10 years including the Berkshire Street Railway-North Adams to Bennington, and the Western Mass line to connect the Springfield and Berkshire systems (Huckleberry Line). Durkee, White and Towne had worked with Ralph Gillett on the Boston, Rochester, & Eastern.

Money

The Hampden Investment Corp., with Ralph Gillett as President, authorized F.S. Mosley to sell stock to banks and local investors. Three Massachusetts banks that held stock were Commonwealth Trust, Old Colony Trust, and Shawmut. Much of the stock was traced to three Boston Banks and Union Trust, now Bank of America.

Construction Companies

There was several construction companies involved in this project:
- Hampden Railroad Company with Ralph Gillett as President;
- Woronoco Construction Company with Ralph Gillett as President and Archie D. Robinson, Henry W. Ely, and Joseph A. Skinner. The Woronoco Construction Co. was hired as the general contractor. Woronoco Construction Company relied on several subcontractors for the major portions of the work.
- Clarence W. Blakeslee of New Haven, CT, built the west end rock cuts and heavy work. The superintendent was William Ryan.
- Boston Bridge Works erected the bridges on west end (Bircham Bend).
- Holbrook, Cabot, and Rollins, of Boston, built the east end rock cuts, heavy work, and concrete work, and eight (8) miles from the west end of the Minnechaug Mountain cut to Hampden Junction. The superintendent was A. N. Lafferty. They also built the branch of the Boston and Maine from East Northfield to Brattleboro Vermont.
- Lewis Shoemaker Co, of Pottstown, PA built the bridges on east end (notably the Swift River-Central Vermont Railroad).
- Numerous sub-contractors:
- F. T. Ley Co. was the cement contractor. Fred T. Ley was also on the Board of Woronoco Construction Company. The superintendent was John McDonald.
- Birnie, Adams, and Ruxton of Springfield.

Route Design

For the Hampden Railroad and its modern route, the design of the road needed to consider customer needs and requirements:

The route design is most critical and must consider current technologies, grades, cuts, fills, bridges over roads, railroads, trolley lines, rivers and curves. The railroad can save many dollars by following natural contours over land, typically following riverbeds. The shortest route may be chosen as the least costly; however, the railroad company may wish to take another route past towns, or industries.

The route design included laying out the route including curves and river crossings. Land had to be purchased; houses demolished along with preliminary grading had to be done... Bridges and roads and houses for use during construction and in final use design, including where cuts would be made and where the fill would be dumped and whether the fill would be sufficient for their needs. In order to build the bridges, such as Bircham Bend Bridge, the footings had to be designed and plans for the underwater work in the caissons had to be made. Also final grading had to be laid out and preparation of sites for stations had to be made. Final track would replace the temporary work track and connections to the other railroads had to be planned.

Build the Railroad

In 1890-1891, surveys were made to lay out a route for the Mass Central connection with Chicopee/Holyoke/Springfield. The final route was completed to Northampton.

The Central New England Railroad completed the tracks through Granby and Southwick and opened their connection at Agawam Junction to gain access into Springfield in 1902.

Charles Sanger Mellen, a protégé of financier JP Morgan, was appointed President of the New Haven system in 1903. By 1910, CS Mellen was also appointed President of the Boston & Maine RR while still President of New Haven Railroad. In order to expand his control of New England Railroads, CS Mellen & Ralph Gillett agreed to build the Hampden Railroad in June 1910. This would make a new connection between the major New England railroads. On August 4, 1910, the Boston & Maine directors filed for a certificate of public convenience and necessity to build the Hampden Railroad. On September 20, 1910, the Railroad Board issued that Certificate.

The next step in building the Hampden was to lay out the line, to "fix" the route. On October 10, 1910, the Hampden Railroad had fixed its route through Ludlow, Belchertown, and Palmer. However, Chicopee and Springfield were not as quick to accept the new railroad routes. On January 31, 1911, the Chicopee Board of Aldermen approved what was known as "Route 3B", the route from Grape Street, under these conditions:

The Hampden Railroad shall:

1. petition the Court for changes of grades;
2. provide a foot bridge across the Chicopee River;
3. cover the Montgomery Street overpass for 200 feet;
4. provide water for the bleachery;
5. relocate all water and sewer lines disturbed; establish a station and freight yard in Chicopee Falls, location to be approved by Chicopee authorities.

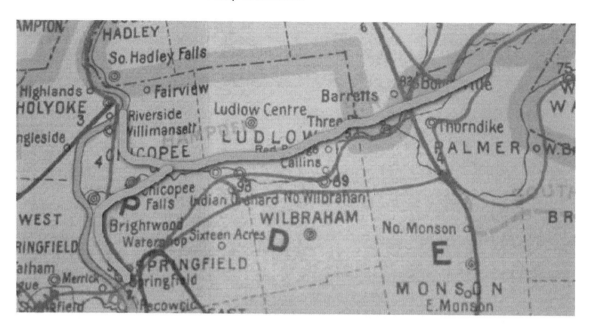

Railroad Locations June 2, 1911 for this Route 3B

Note: The west end connections to Springfield and Holyoke, and connection at east end, Ware River Railroad, not to the Boston & Maine-Central Mass line, (this is an error of the map maker). Map is from 1912 Railroad Commission Report.

As of March 9, 1911, the exact Route was still not fixed into Springfield, two options were:
1. Branch off the Boston & Maine's Chicopee Falls branch by the electric station and go directly south to the Boston & Albany RR to meet at Armory Street. This would follow a natural valley then called the "Atwater ravine", or:
2. Run the route past the Springfield Hospital at the Springfield/Chicopee line. However, this was discouraged due to the many prestigious homes in that area (called Route 1). There were also major concerns about the increased eastbound traffic from the Hampden backing down the New Haven tracks to cross the diamonds to use the Connecticut River line north into both Chicopee and Chicopee Falls.

In March 1911, a 10-year agreement was announced stating that the New Haven Railroad would share the surplus of the Boston & Albany Railroad (including the New York Central lines) and would receive trackage rights on the Boston & Albany lines. Thus, the Hampden could use the Boston & Albany line into the Springfield station. This agreement was to solidify the American controlled lines against the Canadian controlled Central Vermont.

A few days later, the New Haven and the Boston & Maine Railroads announced a new traffic plan to use the Athol Branch to bring traffic into Springfield. The Hampden Railroad would be affected only on its west end, and could connect to the Athol Branch in Ludlow. However, on April 17, 1911, the Hampden Railroad fixed its route in Springfield; this was a changed route from the original March 1911 route to a junction at Athol Junction in East Springfield."[1]

"Building Hampden County Railroad
First Road Constructed By Independent Co. in This State in Twenty
Years Will Cost Over $2,000,000
To Be Important Artery in System of Massachusetts
In this hurry and rush of modern business activity, few people take the time to consider the enormous strides that are being taken by others than their competitors and yet there is construction work going on here in Hampden county that has to do with the first principles in business expansion, the building of a railroad to handle the production of a section of the state that has heretofore had to depend almost entirely upon an artificially created market. This is the first road that has been built in the state in 20 years by an independent company and although its length will not exceed 15 miles it will eventually be one of the main arteries in the Massachusetts system.

The charter under which the road will operate has been granted to the Hampden Railroad company to construct and operate a line from Springfield on a section with the Boston and Albany R. R. East of the Athol branch to a point in Bondsville where it will connect with the Massachusetts Central R.R. on its main road to Boston.

The entire construction work will cost over $2,000,000 and the Company includes a number of [engineers] of local repute. H.S. Durkee of the local firm of Durkee, White & Towne is the chief engineer and is very well known as a man of great ability and one of the foremost railroad engineers in the United States. Associated with construction work is O. E. Parks of Westfield, general manager of the railroad, and an engineer of several years experience.

The engineers have had a great deal to contend with, for the topography of the country does not lend itself readily to construction work of this nature. When it is understood that in the entire distance of 15 miles there are only two curves, both being below five per cent, while other railroads in this section have curves that approximate 10 or even 12 per cent, some idea can be gained of the high degree of technical skill that has been called into play. Added to this the grade had been kept to a maximum of 65 feet to the mile, making possible the carrying of much heavier loads, at a savings of both time and money.

The entire construction work has been {granted} to the Woronoco Construction Co., of Westfield, who in turn, have sub-let the grading work to two different companies, the Holbrook, Cabot, and Rollins Co., of Boston, who are in charge of the western end of the cut, extending from Springfield to the western end of Minnechaug mountain, and the C. W. Blakesee & Sons Co., of New haven, who are doing the work from the other side of the mountain through to Bondsville. The Woronoco Construction Co. is building the culverts and attending to the relocation of the highways.

The route to be followed will be approximately as follows: Branches off the Main line of the Boston & Albany railroad, at a point just east of the Athol branch in East Springfield, the line crosses the

Chicopee River at Bircham Bend, and runs East, passing through Ludlow at the section called Little Canada, and then cutting through the southern end of Minnechaug mountain it makes a northeasterly course through the southern end of Belchertown and up to the township of Palmer, where it crosses the Athol branch of the Boston and Albany R. R., the Central Vermont R. R., and the Swift River and continuing almost due east makes a connection with the Massachusetts Central R. R., about one mile east of Bondsville.

The first work of magnitude starting from the Springfield end will be where the line crosses the Chicopee River. Here a steel bridge is to be constructed, which will join the two banks of the river valley being over 1,055 feet long and over 82 feet in height. It will cross the car tracks and the roads, at a height of over 50 feet, and will be located near the Bircham Bend Power Co's., plant. After crossing the river, the line cuts through the high bank and crosses Fuller Brook, on a fill that will be 75 feet high and over half a mile long. A culvert will be constructed about 204 feet long, with a 10 foot arch, to take care of the water from the brook. The first long stretch of straight track begins here, and will extend for a distance of six miles, to the western end of Minnechaug mountain.

Practically no grading will be done after leaving Fuller Brook, until the line reaches just east of Ludlow. Here it is to cross Woods Pond, on a fill that will be 60 feet high, and over 700 feet long. The pond itself has a depth of 20 feet, and in order to preserve the existing grade, more than 40 feet of dirt will have to be added to the fill in the pond. After leaving Woods pond, the line passes through the Huckleberry Swamp and from there the western end of Minnechaug Mountain is reached, the track will run on a fill averaging 15 feet in height, for the two and one half miles. In some points the height will exceed 50 feet owing to the low lying land that they encountered.

In addition to the big cut, 4000 feet of Three Rivers road will have to be moved to the south, together with the poles and wires of the telephone company, practically all will be new road, calling for extensive grading.

There are at present 12 steam shovels employed on the entire length of the line, all being of the most modern type. The entire equipment, in fact, is the last word in efficiency and demonstrates conclusively the effectiveness with which the railroad builders can utilize machinery in the furtherance of their work. The drills, flat cars, steam shovels, engines, and hand tools in use have been in quite a number of instances, created for the needs that have arisen in the peculiar type of work that they are called upon to undertake, and are monuments to the genius of the American inventive mind."[1]

On April 4, 1911, the Boston & Maine Board of Directors approved a plan to lease the Hampden Railroad, and voted to authorize President Mellen to negotiate the lease.

In late May 1911, the City of Chicopee held a conference to decide whether to use Routes 6B or 3B. The Hampden Railroad wanted to use 3B.

On May 28, 1911 the Chicopee mayor issued the following statement to the Springfield Republican:

"...In connection with this matter, allow me to say that the city of Chicopee does not look with complacency on the effort of Springfield to solve her railroad problems at the expense of our city. The relocation of the Boston & Albany tracks to connect with the Boston and Maine tracks near Brightwood must of necessity traverse one of two routes, one through the Atwater ravine, which involves a long tunnel and which is pronounced impracticable by railroad engineers and the other one over survey No 1 the Hampden railroad. That a railroad in that location would work incalculable damage to the city of Chicopee is the almost universal view of our citizens. The arguments of the Springfield newspapers advocating such a plan are almost amusing in view of their naïveté in forgetting that every argument which applies to the desirability of removing the Boston & Albany embankment from Springfield applies with equal force against locating its embankments and deep cuts in the most available section for home-building in the city of Chicopee..."[4]

This article resulted in the following decisions.

It was decided that using Route 1 would be a bad choice for Chicopee because it cuts across many upscale homes and would join the Boston & Maine at the Chicopee/Springfield line. It was also decided that the Atwater Ravine route was considered impractical by railroad engineers. In order to clear up this route, The Mass. Railroad Commission issued an Order to fix the route in Chicopee on June 2, 1911, (because Chicopee Aldermen could not agree on a route). The Hampden would come into Springfield adjacent to the Boston & Maine Connecticut River main line to Fuller Street (near the Peter Pan bus garage) and follow the Boston & Maine line into the Springfield station.

RAILROAD LOCATIONS

"Petition of the Hampden Railroad Corporation that the Board fix the route of its railroad in the City of Chicopee.

H. W. Ely for the petition
Luther White for the City of Chicopee
It appearing, after notice and hearing, that the directors of The Hampden Railroad Corporation, a corporation in process of formation, has received from this Board a certificate that public convenience and necessity require that a railroad be constructed as proposed in the articles of association of said corporation; that the petitioners have applied, under the provisions of law, for certificates fixing the route of said railroad in the cities and towns named in the articles of association; that they have been and are unable to agree with the aldermen of the City of Chicopee upon a route for said railroad and have not received from them a certificate fixing said route, --it is

Ordered: That the location and route for the railroad of The Hampden Railroad Corporation in the City of Chicopee, as the same is indicated upon a map on file in this office, be as is here described:

Beginning at a point in the center line of the Chicopee Falls branch of the Boston and Maine railroad, said point being about 120 feet easterly from the easterly line of Grape street produced and running thence north 89° 57' east 2,405.6 feet to station 24 + 05.6, thence by a 4° curve to the left to station 39 + 33.1, thence north 28° 51' east to station 55 + 94.00, thence by a 4° curve to the right to station 73 + 06.5, which equals station 75 + 33.12 on continuation of this line, thence south 82° 39' east to station 130 + 65.65, thence by a 2° curve to the right to station 143 + 93.98, thence south 56° 05' east to station 162 + 35.13, thence by a 1° curve to the left to station 167 + 73.13, thence south 61° 30'east to station 203 + 04.08, thence by a 2° curve to the left to station 212 + 04.08, said station equals station 111 + 20 on line from Springfield, Massachusetts, to Hastings Crossing, Palmer, Massachusetts; also being on line between Springfield and Chicopee; thence continuing the same course north 44° 36' E, crossing the Chicopee river to station 94 + 87.41; thence by a 4° curve to the right to station 108 + 84.91; thence south 79° 30' east to station 164 + 50 which equals station 338 + 32 on continuation of this line; said station being on line between City of Chicopee and town of Ludlow.

The above described lines are the center line of location.

The right of way is shown by the lines 100 feet distant from the center line upon each side and parallel with it.

Attest: Charles E. Mann, clerk
June 2, 1911 [8175] pp 227-8

3rd Annual Report of Railroad Commissioners 1912 for year 1911, P 227-8 (this is route 3B, Chicopee station 212 is same a main line station 111)

The Railroad commission approved the establishment of the Hampden Railroad Corporation. Mellen told Gillett that Gillett would receive the contract for building the Hampden. Ralph D Gillett began negotiations with the Boston & Maine Railroad for setting construction prices. Board of Railroad Commissioners 1911, pp 191

The Board of Railroad Commissioners of Massachusetts issued a Certificate of Compliance with Law preliminary to establishment of Railroad under section 24 of general Railroad Laws on June 2, 1911, pp 228

On July 19, 1911 Mellen told the General Auditor of the Boston & Maine to send a letter to Boston & Maine Vice President of Construction, E.H. McHenry, approving Gillett's excavation and overhaul prices:

Earth cut: $0.45 per cubic yard
Rock cut: $1.85
Ballast: $0.60
Overhaul: $0.005 per yard for each station (100 ft) over 500 feet, Board of Railroad Commissioners 1911, pp 191

Mr. McHenry suggested that the Chief Engineer was more knowledgeable on the actual prices for this work. After his inspection of the route, the Chief Engineer recommended these prices:

        Earth cut: $0.375 per cubic yard

        Rock cut: $1.50

        Ballast: $0.60

        Overhaul: $0.0075 per yard for each station (100 ft) over 1,000 feet,
Board of Railroad Commissioners, 1911, pp 192

The Hampden Railroad Corporation petitioned the Railroad Commissioners for a Certificate Preliminary to Location and Construction of Railroad under section 71 General Railroad Laws on August 17, 1911, granted same day. pp228, 229

Petition of the Hampden Railroad Corporation for certificate, under the provisions of section 71, part II, Chapter 463, Acts of 1906, preliminary to construction.

"By order of the Board of Railroad Commissioners I, the undersigned, Clerk of said Board, under the provisions of section 71 of part II, chapter 463 of the Acts of 1906, hereby certify that The Hampden Railroad Corporation has submitted to the Board a sworn estimate by its chief engineer of the total cost of constructing its railroad, other than branches, located in the counties of Hampden and Hampshire, and that said estimate has been approved by the Board. I further certify that it has been made to appear to the satisfaction of the Board that an amount of capital stock of said corporation, equal to at least fifty per cent of such estimated cost, has been subscribed by responsible parties, without any condition which invalidates the subscription, and that twenty per cent of the par value of each share had been actually paid in. And I also certify that the Board has ascertained that the authority and consent required by section 82 of part II, chapter 463 of the Acts of 1906, for the construction of said railroad across the highways and other ways within the counties in which said road is located, have been obtained.

                                 CHARLES E. MANN,

    August 17, 1911   Clerk"[2]

43rd Annual Report of Railroad Commissioners 1912 for year 1911, pp 228, 229

At this same time the lease agreement was drawn up between the Hampden and the Boston & Maine. This was approved by the Boston & Maine Board of Directors in September 1911.

In August 1911 the Hampden petitioned the Railroad Commission for a permit for the location of the railroad, this petition was approved.

At this same time, Gillett formed the Hampden Investment Company to finance the construction. The initial stock of $1,400,000 was held by the Investment Company. Mr. Mellen gave an introduction of Mr. Gillett to Mr. Mosley's investment company for the sale of those stocks.

This agreement was for the Hampden Railroad to construct a road from Bondsville to connect with the Chicopee Falls branch and, when requested by the Boston & Maine, to connect to the Athol branch of Boston & Albany in Springfield. This shall be a first class railroad, laid out for the ease of double tracking, and all work

Philip E. Johnson

done to the satisfaction of the Boston & Maine and approved by the Railroad Commission. The cost of the line to be specified by Gen auditor-Boston & Maine and stock and bonds issued by the Boston & Maine to cover this and assumed by Boston & Maine as shown in the lease. The agreed rental would be interest on bonds, 5% on the stocks, and $500 in expenses. This contract was signed by Mellen and Gillett, and ratified by Boston & Maine stockholders in October 1911.

An agreement drafted between the Hampden Railroad,-Woronoco Construction Company was based on the above prices +10%... The Boston & Maine Railroad General Auditor sent a copy of this agreement to Mellen on August 4, 1911, which Mellen approved.

Meanwhile, the Boston & Maine Railroad General Solicitor and General Counsel for Hampden Railroad sent Mellen a draft of the lease for the Hampden Railroad-Boston & Maine Railroad. And on September 5, 1911 the Boston & Maine Board of Directors voted to lease the Hampden Railroad:

"Voted, that the president be authorized to execute an agreement for a lease of the road, franchises and property of the Hampden Railroad Corporation, upon substantially the terms set forth in an agreement marked 'Agreement for lease, Boston and Maine Railroad and the Hampden Railroad Corporation'" herewith submitted and to be filed with the vice-president in charge of accounting."[2] pp192

This agreement was for the Hampden Railroad Corporation to construct the railroad from Bondsville to connect with the Chicopee Falls branch, and when requested by the Boston & Maine, to connect at the Athol branch of the Boston & Albany in Springfield. It also allowed the company to issue bonds to cover the costs, set forth in the lease conditions for the Boston & Maine. The road would be a first-class railroad, constructed as a single track line, with the track laid to allow double tracking in the future. All work was to be done to the satisfaction of the Boston & Maine. The cost was to be specified by the Boston & Maine general auditor. A draft of the lease was attached to that contract. This contract was signed by Mellen for the Boston & Maine, and Gillett for the Hampden Railroad Corporation.[2] pp 193

This lease was unanimously approved October 11, 1911 by a majority of the Boston & Maine stockholders.

A construction contract between the Hampden Railroad and the Woronoco Construction was executed about same time.[2] pp. 193 & 229

While trying to fix the route into Holyoke, on September 10, 1911, the Hampden Railroad filed a petition with the Holyoke aldermen for route of Branch.

Gillett then organized the Hampden Investment Company with himself as president, to finance the Railroad. On September 26, 1911, Mellen gave a letter of introduction of Ralph D. Gillett to FS Mosley including the following paragraph:

By agreement with the board of directors the Boston & Maine is to take a lease of the property when completed, guaranteeing interest on the bonds and five per cent upon the capital stock.[2] pp 194

"Soon afterward, on October 11, 1911, Mosley agreed to loan Hampden Investment Company $1.4M at a brokers fee of 0.5%, the loan matured on January 15, 1913 and was to be discounted at 4-1/2 percent. Hampden Investment Company was to pay $207k on January 1, 1912 and the Boston & Maine was to certify the work was performed to their satisfaction every 3 months

16

thereafter. The letter was approved for the Boston & Maine by C.S. Mellen, President. The loan was financed by a Boston bank[2] pp194.

Mosley sells notes to various savings banks around the State. The 'Boston Morgan Interlocking Banks' namely the Old Colony Trust, the Commonwealth Trust and the Shawmut National, heard their master's voice from New York through Mellen, and went into the Hampden proposition, heals over head without investigating its merits and without taking proper precautions for their own protection[5] The investment company held practically all of the $1,400,000 in capital stock.[2] pp 194.

Since this money was now in hand, The Hampden Railroad began to purchase land and right of ways beginning with hiring engineering, and all other staff required to build the railroad. The Woronoco Construction sublets some large construction work to two subcontractors: Holbrook, Cabot & Rollins, and C. W. Blakeslee in late 1911. The bridge work was also sub-let. The remainder of the construction work was performed by Woronoco's workforce. Woronoco also provided engineering staff to oversee all sublet work.

Construction work was supervised by the Hampden Railroad engineers, who also calculated the excavation yardage and classification. This was checked every 3 months by Arthur B Corthell, the Chief Engineer of the Boston & Maine Railroad, who calculated the progress of work and estimated the amount of excavation. After an inspection in 1911, the Boston & Maine chief engineer sent a letter on November 14, 1911 to Gillett that the specifications for the railroads' cuts, width, and grades, didn't appear wide enough for double track. The cuts appeared to be only 18 feet wide, not as wide as he assumed was needed for standard width.

Mr. Corthell then gave Ralph Gillett a change order from 18 foot width to 22 foot widths cuts and fills, with 1½ to 1 % slope. Sometime later, Mr. Corthell recommended cuts at 32 feet for better drainage and subsequent double track and masonry should be made for double track. Corthell considered the masonry to be acceptable for double track. As the result of these changes it was estimated that the cost of the road was increased by about half a million dolloars"[2]. pp 195

As the work progressed, some additional capital was secured by F.S. Mosely and notes from the Hampden Railroad Company to the amount of $2,500,000. These notes were held by various banks around Massachusetts. A newspaper reported in December 1911 that C.W. Blakeslee was laying two miles of temporary track from and Boston & Albany tracks to the Minnechaug mountain site, and began placing steam shovels at the site. C.W. Blakeslee state they would not use horses for this project. Also, a local contractor, Birnie, Adams, and Ruxton of Springfield, did some cement and bridge work.

On January 15, 1912 the promoters of the Hampden Railroad asked the aldermen to permit the relocation of the proposed Hampden tracks in East Springfield for a distance of about 1,500 feet. This would relocate the tracks about 350 feet from the present Athol branch near the connection with the main line of the Boston & Albany. This would require the relocation of the Athol branch tracks to parallel the Hampden tracks. They would keep the current Athol branch tracks for freight purposes. The Hampden and Athol tracks would parallel each other and then meet near the signal tower at the junction of the Athol branch and the B & A main line. The petition was granted on January 16, 1912. A large article in the Springfield

Union on February 13, 1912 describes the new road, and mentions a construction track on Three Rivers Road in Ludlow from the Athol branch (west of Minnechaug cut). The prose of the following excerpts describes the changes that are happening.

"The winter sleep of the remote hamlet that one meets in the region between this city and Bondsville is broken by the railroad builder. From early morning until late at night, all through this region, the quiet of which is seldom broken, one hears a multitude of noises. The whistle of a construction locomotive, the sounds of the steam shovels, and the hammer of the steam drills, all blend with the shouting of men and the squeaking of wagons, all signifying the presence of the railroad builders. The distance one sees the faint haze that marks the presence in another place, of that force that is slowly but surely changing the typography of the country, cutting down the hills, filing the valleys and bridging the streams, aided in its work by the most costly modern machinery…

CHAPTER THREE

DESIGN AND SPECIFICATIONS OF THE RAILROAD

The engineering firm in charge of the railroad line has an enormous job, rarely seen or appreciated by the public. A Springfield firm, Durkee, White & Towne, was chosen to engineer the Hampden Railroad. Durkee, White & Towne had its offices in the Patton building on Hampden Street in Springfield. This building is still standing today.

The engineers must design the line using the least costly route by following natural contours of the land. They must decide the route that will cost the least, considering land taking, modification of the land (cuts and fills) to maintain a low grade, few curves, construction of bridges, and labor costs to accomplish the route. In the Hampden's' case, they chose the shortest distance method, to keep a low grade, and only allowed two major curves in the route. However, this route required three major cut/fill operations.

Mr. Henry S. Durkee, the senior engineer on this project, was a very well respected engineer with many years of experience.

Durkee, White and Towne's design included the layout of the road curves, river crossings, and road crossings. Large bridges were necessary for the river crossings, road, railroad, and trolley crossings. Small cement culverts were used for the various brook and stream crossings.

Bridges, where necessary, must be as short as possible, at right angles to the obstacle.

The crowning achievement of the Hampden is the Bircham Bend Bridge, which crossed a road, a trolley line, and the Chicopee River. Its span was 1,100 feet at a height of 80 feet. This bridge also had a clear 300-foot span over the river, meaning it did not have piers or footings in the middle of the river.

The Hampden has 29 bridges listed in Appendix B.

The specifications for the Hampden Railroad required low grades eastbound of 1.23%; and a low curvature of 4 degrees was required for high speed travel. A new Federal Grade Crossing elimination rule caused highway and railroad grade crossings to be avoided. This new regulation required many bridges for overpasses or underpasses, due to the route being placed in populated areas. The Hampden had 28 bridges. This new regulation also required no railroad grade crossings, and the relocation of the Athol branch to the east to avoid a crossing. Only single track was laid. This track was labeled as the southerly line and is at the center of the property line. This method would allow the double track design to be used and a second track could be added without extra design work.

Ralph D. Gillett may have made a lot of money purchasing the land from the owners and then selling it to the railroad company at a considerable profit.

Photo 345: Zabek house being moved from the Hampden
right of way near Chicopee Falls Road, Author's collection

"Ludlow Man Won't Let Hampden Railroad Move His Home

LUDLOW-June 18-A short war occurred this morning near the scene of operations on the Hampden railroad when Frank Buckwheat, residing in the Holyoke road, drove off a number of laborers when they endeavored to begin operations for moving his residence. It is claimed that the company has offered to pay $1500 for the land which they will have occasion to use and will also move his residence while Buckwheat is holding out for $5000, which he considers a fair price. When the men started moving their implements on his property, he warned them off and sent at once for his lawyer."

Photo 408: The Buckwheat home on Holyoke Road in Ludlow. Note the Hampden's grading on the right side of the picture. Author's collection

Survey Team

The route must be determined with cost and character of the railroad in mind.

A reconnaissance was made under the direction of a civil engineer; Mr. Durkee was the Chief Civil Engineer.

The civil engineer plots the line on his map and lays out preliminary stakes for the survey team.

THE RECONNAISSANCE. -THE FIRST STEP IN RAILWAY CONSTRUCTION.

In locating a new railway line or extending an existing one, many factors must be taken account of, such as the cost of the proposed line considered in relation to its probable revenue; the cost of operation and maintenance; and the financial resources of the owners. From an operating point of view it is desirable that the route shall be as direct as possible, a straight line drawn between the termini would be the ideal, but other considerations intervene, such as the most effective and profitable service that can be rendered the population within the territory, the cost of construction first and the expense of maintenance and operation afterward, the effect of the competition of existing or possible lines or other forms of transportation, etc.

When it is desired to construct a new line between given points or extend an old one to a certain point, the first things to know before it can be determined upon are, what will be the best route to take, and the probable cost and character of the road required. To ascertain these it is necessary that the country to be traversed should be examined by engineers. This examination is called a reconnaissance, and is made under the direction of a civil engineer. It is of a preliminary character only it is not intended to give an accurate survey of the country. It is made to determine: (a) an approximate location for the proposed line; (b) that it is possible to ascend from a valley on a given grade, and get over the summit of the divide that it is possible to descend from this divide and cross the summit of the next on a given grade; (d) the elevation of the passes of the divides to the right and left, and (e) that the road can be built within certain limits of expenditure.

The method of making the reconnaissance differs, of course, according to conditions. If the country proposed to be traversed is well known and has been settled, accurate maps and surveys of it can be readily obtained. Accordingly, the engineer provides himself with a map made preferably on the scale of one inch to a mile. Such a map, where a government survey has been made, will give the township and section lines; generally the sub-division of each section by farm fences enables any desired point to be accurately located. [5] pp 47

The reconnaissance results are included in the preliminary survey (1 inch to the foot), which results in the location (final) survey.

This is a rough survey only and not an accurate survey of the country.

If the area is known and maps available from government, the maps can be used to perform the preliminary layout. The Engineer then travels the country by foot to locate the controlling points. Note: The engineer probably would have traveled by horse or foot in 1911, but may have used an automobile wherever possible.

After the recon and preliminary surveys, the location survey is next. The team operates in much the same manner as the preliminary team, but is much more detailed. The survey party will lay out spiral curves in detail and will place stakes in the ground in a small clearing at 100 foot intervals. Station numbers are marked by the team on these stakes. The 100 foot length is due to the length of the measuring chain. This chain is further backed up by a one hundred foot steel tape. The company photographer, Smith of Westfield, used these station numbers to mark his photos.

My photos are marked with station numbers, some examples are:
- Station 0 is at Athol Junction of Boston & Albany
- Station 81 is at the Bircham Bend viaduct
- Station 794 Swift River Bridge
- Station 910 Boston & Maine connection
- See also Appendix B

Now, that the route has been located, the real estate agents can secure the Right of

Way, and the chief engineer can begin the field work with his clerks and draftsmen.

The assistant engineer with his rodmen and chainmen will:
- Check the alignment and locations of hubs and stakes
- Reference the hubs for roads, and borrow pits, etc.
- Re-run all levels, and check benchmarks and elevations.
- Set out stakes for excavation widths and embankments.
- Plan when work must begin on each section.
- Examine the right of way for road and stream diversions.
- Plan for bridge and culvert openings.
- Prepare the Bill of Materials for the bridges and openings.

[5] pp94

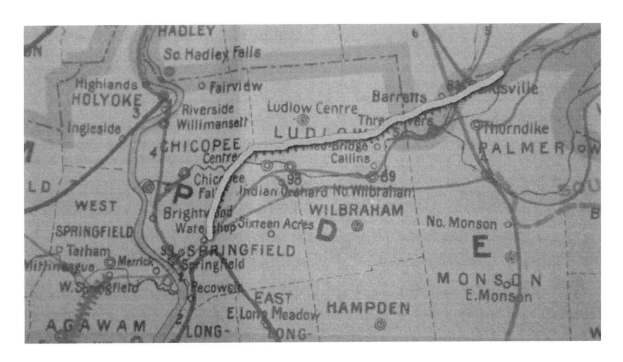

The Final Route 1913

Mass Railroad Commission report for year 1913, Steam Railroad map

SPECIFICATIONS -- Concrete Culverts

Type	Station#	Photo#	Location
Concrete	112	675	Fuller Road Mass Pike
Pipe	214	337	Ludlow
Pipe	154	341	Ludlow
Highway	671	729	by Alden St, Ludlow
20' concrete	679	399	Broad Brook, Ludlow
20' concrete	679	415	Broad Brook, Ludlow
20' concrete	679	421	Broad Brook, Ludlow
20' concrete	679	445-8	Broad Brook, Ludlow
20' concrete	679	728	Broad Brook, Ludlow
Concrete-2 pipe	698	732	Palmer
Concrete	721	413	Palmer

FENCES

The fence posts were made of reinforced cement and placed 16 feet apart along both sides of the right-of-way. The heavy wire fencing was attached and it gave a right-of-way fence that was indestructible by fire, the common destroyer of railroad fences.

A major reason for fences along the right-of-way was to keep out animals, farmers and other pedestrians. You can find many fence posts still standing today, if you know where to look.

Photo 1033: Men posing with concrete fence posts at the fence plant at station 265, near East St. in Ludlow (now under the Mass Turnpike) Author's collection

AS BUILT SPECIFICATIONS

Track: 16.48 miles of rail, The Hampden used 85 pound rail.

There was 14.82 miles of mainline, and 1.66 miles of side track.

From Hampden Railroad newspaper article (as built):

85 pound rail: 133.571 tons/mile, 30' length = 352 per mile

Spikes: 4 per tie, 4x45, 288= 181,152 ref appendix F in Kirkman

45,288 Hard Pine ties. 2,748 per mile approximately

6034 **Tie plates** (newspaper notes tie plate on all ties): 2 per tie + switches= include   angle bars, 1408   **bolts, nuts & lock washers**

Fence posts: 16' on centers, entire length of line, most posts at this time were made of wood, these were made of cement at the post plant in Ludlow, by Station #265, see pp 23

Bridges, There were 29 bridges. (List-Appendix B)

Station at Thorndike, 1913, street side view. Charles Fuller photograph, courtesy of Madeline Bowler picture p 57

East Springfield passenger station 1938, Lewis Wroe photo, Bob Buck/George Ford collection.   Look carefully, you can make out the Westinghouse factory in the right background. picture p 58

Grade The steepest grade the same was 1.23 percent was in Ludlow from Wood Pond to Minnechaug Mountain, the same as the Mass Central in Barre.

There were 18,000 cubic yards of concrete.

There was 150 tons of dynamite used.

The cuts included 2,500,000 cubic yards of material of which 1,125,000 cubic yards was rock fill. Newspapers report 25 to 50% expansion of cuts when used as fills.

Fills Covered in Chapter 5, page 41

Curves The curves were at 4 degrees curvature where 8 degrees was standard in the Northeast on other railroads. The plans for the Hampden indicate a 2000' radius on the curves. The longest straight stretch of track is 5 ½ miles it is the longest in the state. The eastbound travel lane of the Mass Turnpike is now on this section of straight track. A 60 mile per hour speed was the expected speed of the road. Note: according to track charts, a 60 mph curve has to be 3 degrees or greater, Hampden Railroad built to 4 degrees.

Signal and Telegraph lines. A newspaper report 8/1913 tells that the Western Union telegraph lines were complete, and the block signaling was to be completed in about 6 weeks (approx October of 1913). Some 24x24 inch footings can still be found today).

CLEARING THE RIGHT OF WAY

1. Clear and grub the right of way, remove stumps and logs.

Photo 438, the land cleared but not yet grubbed. East of Palmer cut. Author's collection

Photo 254: roadbed is cleared and graded, preparing for work track. Station 103 in Chicopee. This location is under the Mass Turnpike in Chicopee, just as the onramp from Route 291 joins the Mass Turnpike. Author's collection

Western New England Magazine February 1912, reprinted by B & M Society and J. R. Greene. Finished track thru Ludlow.   Note: finished ties, tie plates and 4 spikes per rail. This grading is single track wide, contrary to the article below which says it was planned for double track.

{The} "Hampden railroad is laid out as a doubled track road and for almost its entire length although there is but a single line of tracks in place at present. Should traffic demand however it would be a comparatively simple matter to put another set of rails in place and this would only place a slight outlay."   Springfield Homestead, January 3, 1914

Photo 1131: Central Mass underpass, the Hampden went underneath on November 11, 1912. Author's collection

CHAPTER FOUR

THE LIFE AND WORK ON THE RAILROADS

WORKCAMPS

Many of the men who built the Hampden Railroad were not New Englanders so they needed housing. There was a lot of manual labor used on the construction of the Hampden railroad, at times there were 1000 men working. To accommodate this need, work camps were established. There were work camps in the Minnechaug mountain area for the Holbrook, Cabot and Rollins workers and at Blakeslee & Son's east camp. They were the centers of activity. The offices were located here as well as the sleeping quarters of the men and the blacksmith and repair shops. Although the workers were referred to as Italians they were immigrants from many countries enduring the changing New England weather. Large warm roomy bunkhouses were constructed and covered with durable tar paper.

Photo 720: Typical work camp near to the construction. Location is station 762 in Ludlow. Author's collection

Special attention was been given to ventilation and sanitation, and the contractors drilled wells, and secured a pure supply of water for the men. The storekeeper had a large variety of the foods that appealed to the immigrants and everything possible was done to make living as pleasant for the men who did this work as possible because without them the contractor would be at a disadvantage. There were some men that chose not to live in company housing. In order to save the sum paid for the privilege of sleeping in the main bunkhouse (the shanty boss being the soft universally abused and generally distrusted man on the job as far as the laborers were concerned). Several huts were erected in the rear of the main houses on the sunny protected side of a slope making them warm and weather proof thereby securing the greatest natural protection from the weather. Their sides were set deep in the ground and the huts were made of boards of different sizes nailed together.

The hard-working laborers who lived in these camps wore a smile on their face, and dressed in colorful mismatched clothing, composed primarily with the idea of earning as much as possible. As a result, if it were not for the easily detected features of the race, the workers would be lost in the bundle of varied-hued clothes that they wore. Many of the roads they traveled had never been traveled by anyone but New Englanders. They made themselves at home. The immigrants did a good job, and they liked the work because it was steady and the opportunity to work overtime during the summer.

"The Minnechaug mountain camp of the Holbrook, Cabot, and Rollins has located the repair and blacksmith shops and the dining room for the engineers in charge of the work. At the eastern end of the mountain the CWB have established their headquarters. Here is also a big camp for the laborers, many of whom live in their own individual shanties, preferring to pay their own way than to be under the jurisdiction of the shanty boss in the main bunkhouses. These bunkhouses resemble the quarters of a lumber crew. Bunks are built along the walls in tiers of three, about 14 men living in each house. In the center of the floor is a huge stove, that quickly heats the room, even in the coldest weather. Lamps are hung from the ceiling and at night the men can be seen reading, and smoking and playing cards before turning in. In the morning at the call of "roll out" the bunks are quickly emptied and the men file into the cook house for "grub pile". The man in charge of the bunk house is called the "bull cook", and sees that everything is kept clean, the wood and coal box filled, the lamps trimmed, and the camp is kept up to the standard." [6]

Photo 719: F. T. Leys camp in Palmer at station 900 near Hampden Junction. Several concrete culverts were built here under the Hampden and the Boston & Maine Central Mass. branch. The men are hard at work and the super is on the phone, Photographer posing in doorway. Notice the photographer's box on the barrels. Author's collection

Photo of work camp for Holbrook, Cabot and Rollins in Palmer taken March 18, 1912. Author's collection

ON THE JOB INJURIES

These were hard times for employees. There was no workers compensation insurance in this time period. If you were hurt you might never be able to earn a wage again. You could sue your employer but you probably did not have the money for an attorney and there were no guarantees you would win. Here are a few of the events that took place during the construction of the Hampden Railroad.

On May 14, 1912 at 9:00 a.m. a dummy engine and three cars fell over a three-foot embankment near Sewell Street in Ludlow. The engineer was badly shaken up. The engine was traveling at 4 miles per hour on temporary track when it suddenly gave way throwing the engine and the first three cars down the embankment completely demolishing the cab on the engine. The embankment had not been propped or trussed up, so that the weight of the train caused it to cave in. Thirty laborers were immediately dispatched to the scene of the accident where it took them until 5:30 p.m. to right and relay the tracks. The engine and cars were badly damaged and would delay construction but they were thankful the engineer and the brakemen aboard the train were not injured. Springfield Union May 15, 1912

On the evening of May 21, 1912 in Ludlow, the night watchman on the upper end of the Hampden had a painful experience while joy riding in one of the dummy engines that ran on the narrow gage track. While patrolling along the embankment "he was suddenly seized with a tremendous thirst and the nearest place a thirst of this nature can be quenched is at the camp on the lower end, he decided to repair there at once. Owing to the severe rains walking was difficult and when he arrived at an engine lying unused on the track he decided that the trip would be much quicker if he put the engine into service. After he steamed the boiler he thrust the lever and was soon underway until he struck an embankment that had been weakened by the rain and the extra weight of the engine caused a cave-in and the engine and the engineer both made a few turns and landed at the bottom of the gully. When the watchman righted himself he resumed his patrol, although badly bruised. On Saturday morning he went to bed, where he was laid up for a few days. The engine was righted the next day but had to be out of service for quite a while because of the damage. The newspaper reported that bets were being taken at 100 to 1 that the watchman would not show up on payday to collect his wages. Springfield Union, May 23, 1912

Photo 396, station 872 in Palmer: 2 boilers operating for steam, steam tractor on left. Location is near the Palmer cut west of Hampden Junction. Author's collection

On May 12, 1912 Archibald McLaller injured when he fell thru staging.

On May 20, 1912 Edward McGerra of Three Rivers, was buried in a cave-in, he was rescued.

On June 21, 1912 Frank E. Bowie, 44 was killed near Fuller crossing on the Bondsville Road. He was assisting in loading planks on a car, and was standing part way up the car. A plank fell and knocked him from his footing. He fell to the ground and struck on his head, killing him instantly, his skull being fractured. In addition to a concussion of the brain, he received a broken shoulder and jaw. He leaves a wife and seven children.

On August 2, 1912 an Italian workman had his right foot crushed while attempting to board one of the "dinky" engines. He was standing on a pile of coal, and when the engine was about to pass he tried to board it, but lot his footing, his right foot going under the wheels of the engine. The fact of his being injured was not known for some minutes afterwards when another engineer saw him by the track. He was taken to a Springfield hospital, where it was found necessary to amputate the leg below the knee.

And why is it when there are large groups of men or women together for long periods of time an altercation will break out. The railroad camps were the same.

On December 2, 1912 James Walsh, a foreman of the Hampden Railroad was at home nursing a badly battered head, the result of an assault by one of the employees under him. The cause of the altercation was not known. The Assailant picked up a large stone and struck Walsh several times on the head before he stopped. The men were finally separated and the fellow who did the assaulting skipped. Walsh did not appear to be seriously injured but the next morning his head began to swell and there were indications of a fractured skull. He was sent to his home in New Haven.

On January 31, 1912 Two men were taken to Mercy Hospital one with three bullets in his body and the other badly carved up during a social function at the camp following payday. The men hurt in the disturbance were Calasantis Angelo and Maria Mocci. Calasantis was shot and Maria was stabbed. Both men were expected to recover. They were both arraigned and held on $500 bail. On February 14, Calasantis died. The third person in the fight was Solli Querino.

On March 17, 1913, Patrick J. Gloste had his finger caught in some machinery and it was amputated it at the Ludlow hospital by Dr. Trelehler.

WAGE STRIKE

Track Gang

On June 19, 1912, a story in the Springfield paper related that three men rioted on the Springfield/Chicopee line. They wanted $2.00 per day, from the $1.75. The riot died a quiet death before police arrived. "Sixty Italians* employed by the Woronoco Construction Company in constructing the Hampden Railroad at Red Bridge struck yesterday afternoon for an increase of wages and shorter hours. Chief Consedine and a number of assistants were called to preserve order. The cause of the strike was failure to grant the demand of the Italian laborers who wanted 20 cents an hour. The contractors had been paying $1.75 for 9.5 hours, and the wages were increased to $1.80 beginning yesterday. The other workmen were satisfied with this increase, but the Italians interfered with them, and it was necessary for Chief Consedine to arrest six of them. They were brought down on the afternoon Athol passenger train and lodged in the Ludlow police station, and will be given a hearing before Judge Birnie this morning.[3]

* for clarification, during this time period, "Italians" were immigrants from any country. They were just dumped into one group called Italians.

There were up to 1,000 men combined working on all locations

Payday in Palmer
Photo credit: Charles Fuller photo, Madeline Bowler collection

Paymaster is on the handcar. The men are lined up for pay. The Paymaster was in Palmer making his rounds with Police Chief Timothy J Crimmons who is watching at a distance. The location is likely to be near the Central Mass underpass in Palmer.

Average Day's Work for one Man. The following is a list of the various kind of labor connected with track work, and gives the amount of each which a good man can perform in one day. This will serve to show the relation existing between the labor of one man and a gang of men at any of the different kinds of work specified:

In one day, one man can:

- Place on a grade one-eighth of a mile of ties.

- Spike one-tenth of a mile of track laid on soft ties.

- Spike one-fourteenth of a mile of track laid on hard ties.

- Splice and bolt one-sixth of a mile of track.

- Clean with a shovel one-eighth of a mile of average weeds.

- Unload 10 cars of gravel.

- Unload 8 cars of dirt.

- Load upon cars, 18 to 24 cubic yards of gravel.

- Load upon cars, 20 to 25 cubic yards of dirt.

- Load coal into buckets for engines, 15 to 20 tons.

- Unload coal into sheds, 25 to 30 tons.

- Put into dirt ballast track, 20 new ties.

- Put into gravel ballast track, 15 new ties.

- Put into stone ballast track, 8 to 10 new ties.

- Do labor equal to ballasting 60 feet of gravel ballasted track.

- Do labor equal to ballasting 35 feet of stone ballasted track.

- Chop 2 cords of 4 ft. wood.

- Make 15 to 25 hard wood ties.

- Make 35 to 40 soft wood ties.

- Sixty men can lay one mile of track in a day.

SOURCE: Intl. Textbook Co. Scranton, PA, published as Textbook on Civil Engineering, Colliery Engineering Co, copy courtesy Railroad Extra website.

Photo 304 -- typical work crew posed while taking a break from clearing and grubbing taken March 30,1912 at station 784 near North St/Railroad St., Palmer.

Photo 359: work track laid quickly on temporary ties. People who saw this doubted that the railroad was first-class and newspapers reported this also. Location is station 150 in Ludlow, under the Mass Pike today. Author's collection

CHAPTER FIVE

CUTS and FILLS

HOW TO MAKE A ROCK CUT

- Earth cuts are made by drill, shovels and by hand.
- Set up a steam boiler plant, need boiler tender, fuel
- Steam hammer team bore deep holes into rock
- The dynamite team packs the holes with dynamite. Three hundred thousand pounds of dynamite was used. Then they set off the dynamite.
- One of the mechanical tools of the day was steam drills, precursor to the modern pneumatic jackhammer. These were drills powered by steam and were used to drill holes in the rock the dynamite to blast the cuts.
- Dump cars filled by steam shovel with rock debris and moved by rail to fill areas.
- Clear away debris using train dump cars, move and dump debris to "fill" areas
- Drill, blast, clear until hole is desired width and depth

Ref: article on Dynamite drills: Springfield Homestead, Saturday March 2, 1911:

"At the western end of the mountain, the Holbrook, Cabot, and Rollins Co. have a big undertaking on their hands. The cut that is being made averages more than 50 feet in depth running at times over 80 feet with 10 to 40 feet of solid rock in the bottom that will have to be blasted out. The entire cut through the mountain will be about a mile long, and it is here that the great usefulness of the steam shovels and dynamite drills becomes apparent. Owing to the fact that the ground is so badly frozen, it has been found necessary to use dynamite in small quantities to prepare the way for the steam shovels. The drills that are used are worked from a gasoline tractor, and if necessary, can go down to a depth of 950 feet, although at present, a depth of 20 feet has been found to be sufficient to loosen the earth. Following the drill, come the big 110 ton steam shovels. These are operated on regular railroad tracks, the rails extended as the shovel moves forward. Taking four and one half cubic yards of earth at a cut, the shovel is lifted and swung to one side and dumped into a train of flat cars that are on the bank above the cut. These cars are of a new type of construction that can be dumped simultaneously from the engine. As fast as the train is filled, another takes its place, there is no need to delay the work. A big crew of men is kept busy freeing the track from the dirt that spills from the cars and clearing the way for the shovel. The work on this section is under the supervision of Superintendent A. N. Lafferty and the engineering work is handled by William Johnson, an assistant of Durkee, White, & Towne." [1]

"The total yardage of the excavation is 2,500,000 cubic yards and of this huge bulk, 50 per cent., or 1,125,000 cubic yards because of the 40-50 per cent. Expansion undergone by excavated rock when placed as filling. It is this greater bulk which excavated rock occupies when put into a fill that made possible the widening of the fills on the line to double track width. The total yardage of the concrete used in bridge piers and abutments and in culverts is 18,000 cubic yards. Thousands of feet of highway have been relocated in order to secure the elimination of all grade crossings." Western New England Magazine February 1913.

Photo 403: Blakeslee's Marion model 60 steam shovel at work in the Belchertown cut. Author's collection

Photo 691: work track at station 864 Palmer, west of Central Mass bridge.
Author's collection

Photo 412: steam boiler set up to provide steam for drills to drill blast holes in rock.
Dynamite team pack holes with dynamite. Station 740-west of South Liberty street,
Belchertown. Author's collection

Photo 601: Steam drill gang hard at work in the Belchertown cut.   Author's collection

Steam shovels scoop up rock debris and moved by work trains to the fill areas. Clear away debris using train dump cars, move and dump debris to "fill" areas There were 14 steam shovels at work, built by Marion and Buycrus, some had up to 80 ton capacity per shovel. Construction companies used small railroads with hundreds of cars, sometimes narrow gage, to carry away the rock scooped up by the steam shovels. This rock was then dumped nearby in a fill area. Before cuts were made, a place very nearby had to be located to be use to deposit the material removed (commonly called "backhaul"). Ideally, the material removed from the cuts will be consumed by the fills. Formula for cut vs. fill is cut = 1.5 x fill.

"no trouble disposing of earth and rock excavated for elevations since the specification call for 20-50 foot fills." Springfield Daily Republican, December 8. 1911

Photo 984: Steam shovel hard at work moving rocks in Belchertown cut.
Author's collection

Photo 985: top view of rock cut, station 742. Author's collection

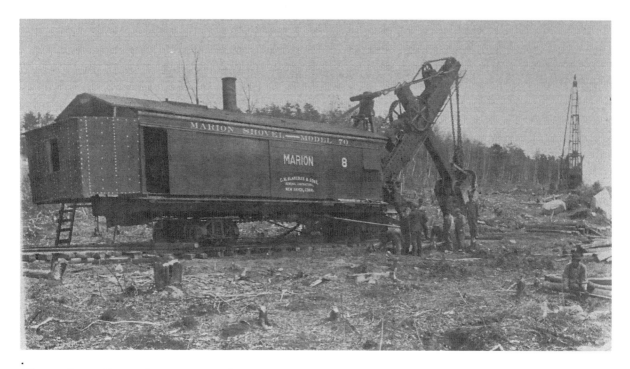

.
Photo 294: One of 14 steam shovels working on the project, Marion model 70, is #8, owned by Blakeslee construction. Author's collection

Drill, blast, clear until hole is desired width and depth. There were three big cuts: Minnechaug Mountain, Belchertown, and Palmer.

HOW TO ADD FILL TO RAISE THE GRADE OF THE LINE.

A temporary trestle using wooden bents and planks or trees had to be set up. Then they would lay temporary railroad track on top of the trestle. Narrow gage track and equipment was usually used, because it is light weight equipment, lighter timber is needed.

Fill dump cars at cuts and send full dump cars across the tracks and dump the material onto the ground under the trestle

Photo 363, station 830 in Palmer, Station 830 west of Route 181, Palmer. Author's collection

It is best to use rocks to fill in under the trestle, because it will not collapse or shift under the large weight of trains like loose fill might with heavy rains. You can cover with loose earth or any material later.

Philip E. Johnson

Photo 971: Note the double set of temporary trestles. The lower level is used to move material, while building and filling under the upper and final level. Location is station 445 in Ludlow just east of the Mass Turnpike rest area, where the Pike turns southeast. Author's collection

Photo No. 351. Author's collection

Photo 352.   Author's collection

Photo 353: using light construction loco on trestle built of logs, the dump cars deliver fill to raise the grade of the line. Side dump cars are ideal because they can dump on either side of the trestle. This buries the trestle (this is why they used wood and cheap material for the trestle)

Photos 351, 352, and 353 are at the same location, in Ludlow. All are from Author's collection.

Photo 333: using light construction loco on trestle built of logs, the dump cars deliver fill to raise the grade of the line. In Ludlow. Author's collection

Cuts contained 2,500,000 cubic yards of materials.

Fills required more, but the cut material expands 40-50%.
Materials from cuts were backhauled to use as fill
The three big cuts accounted for 1,660,000 cubic yards:

Minnechaug Mountain:	800,000 cubic yards	60% rock
Belchertown:	160,000 cubic yards	
Palmer	700,000 cubic yards	50% rock[18]

Wood Pond in Ludlow was a 700-foot long fill. At places it was up to 70 feet deep, with 20 feet of water and 20 feet of mud to be filled in. Wood Pond required fill 60 feet deep and 700 feet long.

Photo 322: construction across Wood Pond in Ludlow, this area is barely recognizable today, cut apart by Mass Pike interchange #7. Author's collection

Photo No. 321 Wood Pond, Ludlow. Author's collection

Photo No. 348, Looking east over Wood Pond. Author's collection

Photo 1137, Foster Street, relocated and new high way bridge constructed in 1912. Author's collection

Foster Street has been relocated to the north years ago, and this area is greatly overgrown, but concrete and even some wood could still be found in 2007.

Below, is a typical rural dirt road, temporary railroad built overhead, and a small plate girder bridge to be added later.   It is likely to be in Belchertown/Palmer area, on the long fill. Author's collection

Concrete being moved up incline to pour into abutment for road overpass. Author's collection

Photo 675, Fuller Brook in Chicopee, this culvert is still in use today by the Mass Turnpike. It is the longest culvert, 204 feet long with a 10 foot arch It is still easily visible in Chicopee from Shawinigan Drive. Author's collection

This is the bridge at station location 768, which is on "the road to Belchertown"- just west of the Athol branch overpass, This makes this road South Liberty Street.

This is a small stream culvert, location unknown, similar culvert can be found in Ludlow near Tower Road. Author's collection

Page Blvd., Springfield. This is the only 2 span bridge on the line. Note: trolley track in left foreground. Lewis Wroe Photo, Author's collection.

The quote below describes the wooden trestle prepared for the large fill west of the Minnechaug Mountain cut and the fill west of the Mass Central overpass before the Palmer cut. Much of Ludlow fill was used to gain elevation eastbound.

"The 1600 foot trestle at the western end, marks the end of the two and one-half miles fill and the accompanying cut will give some idea of the magnitude of the task in this section alone. The contract of The Holbrook, Cabot, & Rollins, ends at the Minnechaug mountain cut, and is taken up by the Clarence W. Blakesee Co., with Clarence Blakesee and Superintendent William Ryan in charge. Associated with them is Harold Murphy, also of Durkee, White, & Towne, who is in charge of the engineering work. East of the Bondsville to Three rivers trolley line, there is a big trestle and cut of the eastern division. The trestle commences at the eastern end of the big fill and crosses the highway at a height of 40 feet. It extends for 2000 feet and joins the one and one-half mile cut near Bondsville, passing under the Massachusetts Central tracks at a depth of 20 feet, and joining them again a mile further on the east end of the cut. About one half mile of the public highway will be moved to the east so that it will parallel the railroad track". Springfield Homestead Saturday March 2, 1911[1]

CHAPTER SIX

STATIONS

Four stations were built of stucco with red tile roofs. On opening day they were completely ready for travelers. The passenger and freight stations were East Springfield (at the end of Rose St.), and Ludlow (at Route 21 and Sewall St.), while combination stations were in Three Rivers (off Pleasant St.), and Thorndike (by Railroad St.). Artesian wells have been drilled to supply pure water to the stations.

Railroad De Luxe Is Title Given the Hampden Railroad … "They are one-story structures and contain a large waiting room and freight room on the first floor. Ample space has been devoted to each. The waiting room is well equipped and rivals some of the more pretentious stations in fair sized communities. The office of the stationmaster is also thoroughly equipped. The building contains exceptional heating facilities and is lighted by electricity. The spacious walk surrounds it while there is also a long concrete baggage platform at one end. In designing the building allowances have been made for the future and the station will serve the needs of travel on Hampden for many years to come there are similar structures at Belchertown and Bondsville."… Springfield Homestead, January 3, 1914[7]

Completed station at Thorndike, 1913, street side view. Charles Fuller photograph, courtesy of Madeline Bowler

East Springfield Station, Passenger and Freight

At the end of Rose Street and driveway to green building (formerly Northeast Tool). the Hampden right-of-way went on the north side of building and out the gate area. This Author inspected an old foundation, 15 by 21 paces, in the middle of the driveway. This foundation could have been the freight station, as no bay was found for bay window. However, no fence posts or mile marker could be found in June 1981. During the Winter of 1981-1982 the owner removed and paved over the foundation.

This photo of the East Springfield passenger station taken in 1938, by Lewis Wroe is part of Bob Buck/George Ford/Author's collection. If you look carefully, you can make out the Westinghouse factory (demolished in 2012) in the right background.

Ludlow Station, Passenger and Freight

South East corner of Hampden Right of Way and Route 21.

Ludlow Stations June 1913, waiting for a train that is not coming....all dressed up and no where to go.   Woman at right of picture is likely holding a box camera taking a photograph of the man posing in front of the station. Photo from Author's collection.

This photo is looking east, note the side tracks on the left or north side; it appears there is a passenger train on the siding.

Thorndike Combination Station
Thorndike Combination Station was located on Pleasant Street. It remained standing and in use as a residence until the 1990's when Massachusetts Electric purchased the property and razed the structure and subsequently built a power sub-station off Pleasant St just east of mile marker 83. Photo on page 57

Three Rivers Combination Station and Water Tank-

It is located off Railroad Street, Palmer.

The right-of-way went at 90 degrees to road, continued east to Central Vermont and Swift River Bridge at Station 894.

A few years ago, I inspected the old foundation, 18 by 45 paces. The station had a basement. I saw the bay window foundation, the footings, the drain and the water supply tank for the station. Mile marker 82 should be nearby, but cannot be found and is believed to be lost. Water tower was located here because steam locomotives need water every 80-100 miles depending on steam used for grades. This location is 82 miles from Boston. Three Rivers station, taken from Railroad St., overpass, showing water tank.

During the week of May 8, 1913 it was expected that the four stations would be completed, although the line was primarily planned for freight, but it was constructed so that it would be fit for passenger service. It was the best built modern road according to many sources.

Charles Fuller Photo, courtesy of Madeline Bowler, Author's collection

Engine facilities: None, and there was only one water tank, at the Thorndike station. No other facilities existed.

CHAPTER SEVEN

THE BIRCHAM BEND BRIDGE

The first work of magnitude starting from the Springfield end, will be where the line crosses the Chicopee River. Here a steel bridge is to be constructed, which will join the two banks of the river valley being over 1055 feet long and over 82 feet in height. It will cross the car tracks and the roads, at a height of over 50 feet, and will be located near the Bircham Bend power company's plant. Springfield Homestead, Saturday March 2, 1911.[1]

The crowning achievement of the Hampden Railroad is the Bircham Bend Bridge, which crossed a road, a trolley line, and the Chicopee River. Its span was 1,100 feet at a height of 80 feet containing 1429 tons of structural steel. This bridge also had a clear 300-foot span over the river, meaning it did not have piers or footings in the middle of the river.

April 1912 view from the Southern side of the Bircham Bend Bridge location.

Photo 431, Author's collection.

Current view from the Southern side of the Bircham Bend Bridge location. Author's photo

Photo 668: July 1912: Looking south from Chicopee side of river towards Springfield.

Compressed air caissons visible on both sides of the Chicopee River. Author's collection

Boston Bridge Works completed steel work on the bridge. It had 2 river piers, 1 land piers, 2 abutments, and 7 huge steel towers the highest of which is 75 feet. The bridge had 1,426 tons of structural steel. Eight hundred tons were used for the clear span across the river, 300' long 55' deep. This was the deepest bridge in all of Western Mass. The total length of the bridge was 1,098 feet, from abutment to abutment and towered 85 feet above the water. This was the deepest bridge in all of Western Mass.

FT Ley Company performed the concrete work for the footing for the bridge.

Photo 661: July 1912: Compressed air chamber for working underwater, also called a caisson. Author's collection

The engineers determined from borings that the riverbed in the middle of the Chicopee River was not suitable for piers that could support the weight of the proposed bridge. So an alternate plan was created to have large supports on each side of the river to support large bridgeworks that would not have support in the middle of the river. This is called a clear span and will require a large lattice of steel to support the weight of railroad trains. The piers on each side of the river would need to be seated on bedrock, so there would have to be very large piers in the river banks about 300' apart. These were anchored to massive 30x34 foot concrete footings. Men called "sand hogs" worked below the rivers; surface in compressed air chambers called caissons (see photo above). This compressed air method will be used on other bridges and tunnels, but not in Western Mass for several years.

Photo 1055: October 1912: Bridge members stored for Bircham Bend trestle. Author's collection

Photo 964, Boston Bridge Works railroad car crane. Boston Bridge Works completed the steel work on the bridge. Author's collection

STEEL TRESTLES

The general type of construction is shown in Photo 1088 below. "Usually the spans are alternately about 30 and 60 feet without much regard to the height of the trestle; longitudinal bracing is placed under the 30-ft. spans joining the vertical bents in pairs forming towers capable of resisting the longitudinal forces due to starting and stopping trains on the track.

The open deck is carried by the plate girders, spaced to support the ties on the upper flanges; the bents are in vertical planes and the posts batter about 2 ins. per foot. Each post rests on a masonry pier some 4 to 5 ft. square at the top and large enough at the base to reduce the unit pressure on the foundation at a safe value. Anchor bolts are set to the template before the pier is built, and the masonry thus adds to stability in case of wind pressure strong enough to produce tension in the post.

Ordinary bridge abutments are used at the ends for moderate heights..."
pp 229-230[8]

Photo 1088: detail of towers and girder construction at Bircham Bend. Note Boston Bridge Works derrick #5 on the trestle. Author's collection

Station 81 is at the Bircham Bend viaduct, Holbrook, Cabot, and Rollins was the contractor for the west end.

For the Bircham Bend work, temporary construction track was built from Athol junction across the flat unpopulated areas out to the bridge site. This track was placed on the same location as the Hampden main line. It was used to bring the steel to the bridge site, as well as operate the Boston Bridge Works crane.

As with all the Hampden line, this bridge was single track, the cement work was not wide enough for double track, and the incremental cost of bridge steel would be very large.

A bridge of Bircham Bend's size with the expected large volume of traffic needed to be at right angles with the shore. This was determined by direct measurement and triangulation. It was decided to use caissons for footings for the bridge.

"An adz is used to give to the outside walls their proper batter. They are sheathed with 4-inch plank, tongued and grooved, the joints of which are filled with either hot coal tar or pitch. The sheathing affords a smooth outside surface, which greatly reduces the friction of the earth against the sides of the caisson. The timers forming the inside walls and ceiling of the caisson chamber are first thoroughly calked and then covered with a layer of 1-1/2-inch hemlock or spruce. This surface is then covered with tarred paper and a second layer of 1-1/4-inch matched spruce boards, with leaded joints..."The Elements, V2pp 997 – 999 [9]

"In sinking these great masses of concrete, 30 by 34 feet in size, the caisson, or compressed air method, was used for the first time in years in western Massachusetts. The building of this bridge, which is now a landmark visible for miles, was one of the feats of the construction of the Hampden Railroad. The river truss, carried across this river on timber work known as 'falsework,' is all in place. The bridge, practically complete except in a few details, has a high factor of strength and its lines are extremely graceful." Western New England Magazine February-1913.

When the caisson is completed an air hose is still attached to it and is it pushed gently into the water to its final resting place. It is very heavy to move. Once it is in the water, care must be used to direct it properly. Once the air hose is disconnected, it can no longer be moved.

They prepared the riverbed and poured the cement for the bridge works. FT Ley Company performed the concrete work for the footings for the bridge. Borings in the Chicopee River showed poor conditions down to 85 feet, so it was necessary to have two piers in the river about 300 feet apart. These piers were anchored to massive 30x34 foot concrete footings. Men called "sand hogs" worked below the rivers surface in compressed air chambers called caissons (photo 661, Pg 61). This compressed air method had not been used in Western Mass. for several years.

Picture 1081: Bircham Bend Viaduct showing present-day Worcester Street and trolley track. Author's collection

Completed Bircham Bend trestle, detail showing 300 foot clear span of the Chicopee River.   Lewis Wroe Photo, Authors' collection.

In January 2007, I met Tony Noret who worked on dismantling part of the Hampden Railroad. He was a construction contractor in the 1930's. His company was hired in 1935 to remove the big Bircham Bend trestle to salvage the steel. They needed additional approval from the Electric Company before actual demolition. The price of steel had jumped from $5 to $6 per ton, because the Japanese were buying steel before the War. Tony believed that this steel went to Chapman Valve. He estimated they salvaged about 800 tons of steel.

They cut the beams on both sides, and then pulled it over with a bulldozer. Tony remembers a 6-inch main beam that he cut through. Tony noted there was no paint on the bridge, so he didn't need to burn it off. They strung a cable across the river with a winch. Tony was on the South side, on the east side of the big pier when...a cable snapped and lashed back it hit Tony in the middle of his back, it threw him up 50 feet on the bank. (He was lucky to be alive!) The bridge shook and wobbled then fell over.

Tony was delighted to receive a picture of the bridge (the picture below) from me. He seemed a little puzzled, then his eyes lit up and he said, "I was right there" as he pointed at the picture below. He never expected that anyone had a picture. Tony said there was a photographer there to record the bridge drop, but he missed the shot and was so angry that he kicked the camera.

The land piers were already taken down before they got the job to finish the big bridge, Tony believed that someone from Providence RI had that easy job.

Photo on the next page is from Western New England magazine, February 1913.

Philip E. Johnson

CHAPTER EIGHT

THE SWIFT RIVER VIADUCT

The Swift River valley was another obstacle for Durkee's engineers to conquer. In order to maintain the proper grade and elevation, a large fill was needed on the east side of the Swift River and continuing east for a distance. The engineers designed a 40 foot tall bridge and trestle system which was over 700 feet long. This five-span trestle crossed not only the Swift River valley, but the Central Vermont railroad also. This site is approximately 1 mile west of Palmer Street, between the Thorndike and the Three Rivers stations.

In the original photos, the Swift River Bridge is identified as Station 794. Lewis Shoemaker Co. of Pottstown, PA built the Swift River project.

Heavy equipment such as the steam shovels had to be moved by spur railroad tracks from the closest line to work sites. There were no heavy hauling trucks to move these shovels.

A temporary spur was constructed off the Athol branch in Three Rivers (photo 308) to build the Swift River viaduct and have shovels for other nearby work.

Photo 308: temporary sidings built off the Boston and Albany's Athol branch to deliver materials for the Hampden Railroad construction. Looking north. March 1912. Author's collection

The Three Rivers station was just west of the bridge location, on what is now Railroad Street or North Street in Belchertown. The Central Vermont railroad delivered the steel to the site. Steam engines drove the hoisting machines that put the steel in place. Large wooden forms were constructed for the massive cement piers which held up the steel girders.

Many men would have been working at this project, both on the fill operation and constructing the concrete forms and then filling the forms. Afterwards, the ironworkers would erect the steel.

Typical cement crew on the Hampden railroad:

This is how the cement gets into the forms. The cement is poured into the buckets, then hoisted up and dumped in. The seams from the forms at Swift River piers are still easy to see. Author's collection

Photo 305 foot bridge across the Swift River March 30, 1911. Author's collection

Heavy Construction

Photo: Western New England Magazine, February 1913

Same location 2003, farm fields long gone, all woods now. Author's photo

Early view across the valley from the west 1911. Note the foot bridge also seen on page 73. Author's collection

Today's view from the western-most abutment. The power lines follow the right of way and show the height of the fill required to maintain grade. Author's collection

Finished Swift River Project

Photo: Western New England Magazine, February 1913

The concrete footings for the trestle and the tall concrete monuments can be seen today. (Please keep in mind that these are on private property.) There is also a geocache nearby, you will have to find that yourself.

CHAPTER NINE

BROAD BROOK

Workers made cement culverts for small streams. They needed to prepare forms, pour cement, finish work, and finally backfill. "

The course of the large stream was diverted and contained in a 20-foot culvert 140 feet long resting at the base of a 60-foot fill extending about 3,000 feet." Western New England Magazine February 1913 pp11

The widest culvert is this 20' cement arch is over Broad Brook, Ludlow.

Photo 446: Forms being assembled in place for Broad Brook culvert, Ludlow near South Street Cemetery. Author's collection

Photo 399: Work camp at Broad Brook. Author's collection

Photo 445 before forms are built for arch. Author's collection

Photo 728: Completed Broad Brook culvert. Author's collection

Photo 448, also Broad Brook. Author's collection

Crandall & Barnes, P 194 plan for typical culvert: [8]

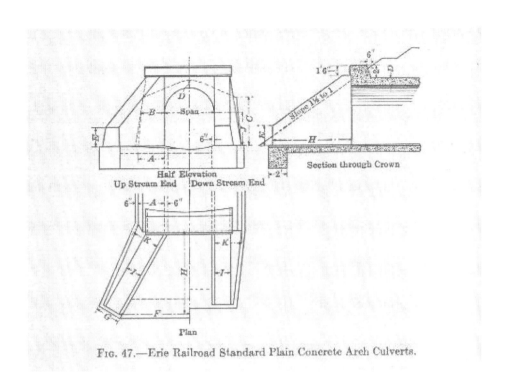

FIG. 47.—Erie Railroad Standard Plain Concrete Arch Culverts.

CHAPTER TEN

OPENING DAY-- THE BEGINNING OF THE END

Newspaper article about 1913 Spring passenger schedule including train numbers and times. See Appendix C for schedule.

Springfield Union on May 8, 1913 on page 4 reported that the four passenger stations would be completed that week and that the road was intended for passenger traffic first and then for freight. It was the best built and modern road in the area.

SPECIAL OBSERVATION TRAIN

Twelve general officers of the Boston and Maine railroad system passed through Springfield on a special observation train yesterday on the way to the north, after inspecting the just-completed Hampden railroad which connects Bondsville and Athol Junction. They stopped in the Union station for a few minutes and posed for the Homestead's photographer. The officials who made up the inspecting party yesterday were photographed at Union station by a Homestead representative and were as follows: Vice-President H. T. Horn of the Boston and Maine company; A. B. Corthell, chief engineer; General manager B. R. Pollock; General Supt. W. F. Ray; Supt. H. J. Robinson; Freight Traffic Manager A. S. Crane; S. A. D. Forristell, Superintendent of Telegraph; C. H. Wiggiris, Superintendent of Motive Power; and others. W. H. Ford, superintendent of the Southern division joined the party here, going over the road with them between this city and Northampton

Boston & Maine Officials On Tour

Group of Magnates Who Inspected the New Hampden Railroad Yesterday

Coincident with their visit, it was unofficially announced that a new passenger schedule for the New Haven railroad, between New York and Boston, will go into effect June 23. This is due to the completion of the Hampden railroad, which is 15 miles long, affording a connecting link between Springfield and the Central Massachusetts Railroad (CM RR), a part of the New Haven system.

These trips of inspection are made from time to time as the general officers think advisable. It is understood this trip was made at the desire of President C. S. Mellen for the purpose of inspecting several new cuts and work of regrading between this city and Boston, and to visit the new stations in East Springfield and at several small places up the river. No further official advices were given by the party in Springfield, but it is understood by the officers, after proceeding as for north as Northampton, will return toward Boston over the tracks of the CM RR or go up through the Hoosac tunnel and into New York state.

Yesterday May 10, 1913 an inspection run from Boston via Central Mass to Bondsville, then slowly to Athol Junction took place. Then via Boston & Maine Conn River line to South Vernon to Dole Junction to Brattleboro, south to Greenfield, and back to Boston on the Fitchburg line. The new schedule begins June 23.

It is an interesting rumor coming from a reliable source in railroad circles that President Mellen was in today's party and that the absence of regular train orders providing for a definite itinerary is due to the fact that the trip is to be shaped by President Mellen as the train proceeds. It is intended however, to have the party returned to Boston no later than tonight.

If Mr. Mellen was in the party he kept himself in careful seclusion within the train while in Springfield. During the stop here the group seemed to be conducted by Vice-President Horn of the Boston and Maine Railroad company. It is remarked that it would not be unnatural for a man who has been so much in the criticism of the public as Mr. Mellen has recently, to prefer to keep out of sight when not inconvenient to do so.

On May 13, 1913 The Certificate for preliminary operation of Railroad was granted.

On July 9, 1913 thirty people from Westfield, Springfield and Ludlow toured the line on July 7th. They left the Woronoco Construction Company offices on Stebbins Street in Ludlow (Holyoke road) and went to East Springfield, then rode to Bondsville Junction. They commented the stations were well built and arranged, floors approaches and platforms were cement, Ludlow even had trees and shrubbery. The Western union telegraph lines were being installed.

"HITCH IN RAILROAD PLANS
HAMPDEN ROAD DELAY START
NO TRAIN SERVICE FOR MONDAY

New Line is Completed and Reasons for Postponement Not Apparent

Regular train service on the new $4,000,000 Hampden railroad will not begin on Monday morning, as was announced some weeks ago by the New Haven railroad company. The new line, which connects with the Central Massachusetts at Bondsville, has been officially inspected by the railroad commission of the state and pronounced good, a certificate granting permission to operate trains over the line has also been issued and the schedule of trains was made up, but it has now become known that the line cannot be in operation on the stated date. Officials in this city will shed no light on the puzzle. W.H. Ford, assistant division superintendent of the Boston and Maine, said last night that the new road would not be opened on time. He stated that he didn't know what the matter was, and had no idea when the train schedule will go into effect. The Hampden road is not to be operated under his supervision.

A rumor that the state railroad commission had refused to allow the New Haven to run fast passenger and heavy freight trains over the line because of poor roadbed was denied last night at the office of the commission in Boston. The commissions local inspection, D.M. Wheeler, said that only yesterday he had made a tour over the Hampden line which is 15 miles long, and found it to be excellent and ready and found it to be excellent and ready for train service. He said he expected the road to go into use on Monday, and know nothing to prevent it.

According to the schedule which the New Haven company announced, six passenger trains daily will operate over the Hampden road West bound they are as follows: No. 1118 arrives in Springfield at 2:45 a.m., No.1501 arrives at 7:25 a.m., No. 1517 at 11:30 a.m., No. 1100 at 1:45 p.m., No. 1520 at 8:45 p.m. and No 1545 at 7:40 p.m. East-bound the six trains will leave Springfield as follows: No. 1114 at 3:25 a.m., No. 1524 at 7:30 a.m., No.1528 at 9 a.m., No. at 2:12 p.m., No.1504 at 5:05 p.m., and 1566 at 5:35 p.m. Four of them are through passengers between New York and Maine. The other two locals running between Northampton and Ware. When the Hampden road train service finally is started passenger rates between local points on the Central Massachusetts will be raised to 2½ cents a mile, which is a slight increase over past rates. The company explains the boost by simply pointing to the immense expenditures which have been made to put the Central Massachusetts into good working condition." pp5 [9]

See the recreated schedule in Appendix D

On the front page of the Springfield Union on June 21, 1913 it read "Boston & Maine Drops Operation of Hampden Line – Announcement from New Haven Railroad Offices Says Road Will Be Abandoned by Subsidiary of Mellen System -- APPROVAL OF LEASE REFUSED BY BOARD – General Manager of Local Line Says Statement Must be Based on Misunderstanding: Parks Hopes for Plan's Consummation."

The Railroad Commission of Massachusetts had refused to grant the lease of the Hampden Railroad to the Boston & Maine on June 20. It was explained that approval of the Railroad Commission was absolutely necessary before the Boston & Maine could operate on the Hampden Railroad. Plans were abandoned for service over the Central Massachusetts over the Hampden Railroad.

The Springfield Union reported on June 24, 1913 that Holyoke's Petition was opposed. Originally the Hampden had been proposed to have a spur through Holyoke which was on the plans as filed. However, the finished route was not completed as filed. At the time of this hearing an additional bond would need to be authorized for this spur to be built because the Hampden Railroad was overextended.

By now the Hampden has caught the attention of many people. A railroad that had seemed to be a good investment in business for Springfield to Palmer was slowly turning into a nightmare. In the Springfield Homestead on Wednesday, June 25, 1913 it announced that the:

"HAMPDEN RAILROAD TO BE PROBED BY THE STATE COMMISSION
Engineers to Make an Appraisal of the Road to Determine the Actual Cost
ASSERTED THAT THE ROAD CAN BE DUPLICATED BY $1,250,000
Story of How This Most Costly Piece of Railroad Construction Carried Out Contrary to the Original Plans—President Mellen Said to Be Power Behind the Throne

The state board of railroad commissioners is about to begin an investigation of the affairs of the new Hampden railroad company, as a result of the disclosures made at the hearing in Boston Monday on the petition of the Hamden railroad corporation for authority to issue additional bonds to the amount of $2,000,000.

It has been represented to the state board that this 15-mile stretch of railway, upon which $4,145,065 has been expended to date, can be duplicated at a cost not exceeding $1,250,000 in order to determine whether this estimate is founded upon fact, and to settle once for all whether or not $3,000,000 has been thrown away in the construction of the road, the state board have decided that a thorough appraisal of the property shall be made by competent engineers, under state auspices, some time this summer.

Particular attention will be paid to this allegation that the rails have been laid on Norway ties, a cheap substitute for oak or chestnut ties, and that the rails themselves are what are known as "'seconds'".

Furthermore, in view of the representation of the officials of the Hampden road that the cost of construction was $250,000 per mile, though the average cost of railroad construction per mile in America is less than $50,000, and keeping in mind the fact that the Lehigh railroad, which presented much more difficult problems of engineering than the Hampden road, was constructed at a cost of only $170,000 per mile, the state commissioners are determined to probe the whole matter of expenditures down to the last dollar.

At the same time, the board will seek to lift the veil of mystery which has shrouded the Hampden railroad enterprise from the start.

It will be recalled that, at the previous hearing in Boston, the fact developed to the very great amazement of the public, that President Gillett of the Hampden railroad was also the president of the Woronoco construction company which built the road under contract, and if immense profits were earned in the building of the road. It was assumed that a generous slice of these profits found their way into Mr. Gillett's pockets.

But who is back of this Hampden railroad enterprise? That's the question which will be fully answered when the probe of the state commissioners shall have been completed. It is rumored that President Charles S. Mellen of the New Haven system was the original author of the Hampden railroad. That railroad was planned before the New Haven railroad was merged with the Boston and Maine railroad, likewise before the New Haven system had acquired by lease the Boston and Albany railroad.

When President Gillett and his associates petitioned for a charter to build in Hampden road, they represented that a '"a present exigency"' required that a connecting road be built between Bondsville and Holyoke, and connecting with Chicopee and Springfield. In their profile map, prepared at the time the petition was granted the road from Bondsville was shown to have two forks branching off at or near Chicopee. One fork proceeded direct to Holyoke; the other fork proceeded to Springfield. But this plan was never carried out in full.

Now mark the course of events. After the construction of the Hampden railroad had been well begun, the New Haven system acquired both the Boston and Maine and the Boston and Albany lines. The early plans for the Hampden Railroad were hurriedly and as far as the public was concerned, secretly changed. Instead of building through to Springfield, as was originally planned, a spur track was cut through at Ludlow connecting with the Athol division of the Boston and Albany, which division had been recently acquired by Mr. Mellen. The branch line to Chicopee and Holyoke was never built, although the promoters of the Hampden railroad assert their intention to build it "some day." Their failure to build the Holyoke connection, which by their charter declaration was needed to supply a "present exigency," has angered the Paper City manufacturers and business men, and they were represented at the hearing in Boston last Monday. All the facts will be reviewed in detail by the state railroad commissioners before granting the Hampden railroad authority to issue $2,000,000 of bonds.

The position of the Boston & Maine stockholders is yet to be considered. A large percentage of the shareholders were opposed to the Boston and Maine merger with New Haven system, and they were absolutely not consulted in the matter of building the Hampden railroad. Yet it is now proposed by Charles S Mellen, who directs the destinies of the New Haven, the Boston and Maine and the Boston and Albany and the Hampden railroad and guarantee a 5 percent dividend on a capitalization of $4,145,685. Some of the largest stockholders of the Boston and Maine view the proposal in a very hostile light and were bitter in their opposition at the hearing in Boston last Monday.

Boston and Maine Opposition

William F. Lawrence of Medford reported to be a large holder of Boston and Maine stock, said it had been the custom of the board for years to require petitioning railroads to file a profile map. He said that he had been unable to find a profile map of this road on file with this board.

"'According to the reports of the interstate commerce commission'" Mr. Lawrence continued, "'the average cost per mile of railroad construction in the country is from $35,000 to $50,000 a mile. This road is asking for an extraordinary thing. If the Boston and Maine is seeking to lease this road, it should be shown it was reasonably necessary to issue such a large amount of stock and bonds. A profit percent of the company's expenditures for the road construction cannot be made without a study of the profile map. Commissioner Prouty of the interstate commerce commission that the amounts were paid were different from those presented here. It is not reasonably possible to determine whether anyone will objct to this issue of stock or bonds on an intelligent basis without having a profile map before him.'"

Where Are The Profile Maps?

Chairman MacLeod thought the request a reasonable one and requested the company's official to present to the board at their earliest convenience a profile map such as suggested by Mr. Lawrence.

Mr. Ely said that such a map has been placed on file with the board, but it was found after a search the plans have not been filed with the secretary of state in accordance with the law.

H.D.O. Kurrie of Boston also made a request for a profile plan. He said that he had been unable to find copies in the office of the railroad commission, and he discovered after a trip to Hampden county that the plans filed there are not consistent with the actual work done by the road. Springfield Homestead, June 25, 1913

Holyoke's Petition in the Matter

At the hearing Monday, City Solicitor Thomas J O'Connor of Holyoke explained that he appeared at the request of Mayor White. His statement follows: "'On the 4th of October, 1910, the usual form of petition was filed by the directory of this road, where, among other things, it requested that hearings, as required by law, be given by the board of alderman. From that time on to the present, nothing has been heard from any director or from the board of directors of the road. It was depicted at that time this railroad was going through the confines of the city of Holyoke. Manufacturers of Holyoke were very much interested in this proposed railroad, and it was expected that the road would go through Holyoke. As a matter of fact, nothing was heard from the time the petition was filed up to the present."'

"'Holyoke desire to enter its protest in this one respect.'" Mr. O'Connor continued, "The petition at the time was filed by the promoters and directors of this railroad really intended and we wanted the road to enter the city of Holyoke. Something further, however, should have been done than to file a petition with the board of alderman. The termini in the western part of the city was to be in Holyoke. The road should have at least asked for a hearing in Holyoke.'"

Henry W. Ely's Statement

Replying to the Holyoke city solicitor Mr. Ely (Attorney for Hampden Railroad) admitted that in the original petition for a certificate of exigency it was proposed to build through Springfield, Holyoke and Chicopee and he contended that the road intends to carry out this plan. "The original idea was as set out'," he said, "it is also the idea now.'" But as we came into this proposition, we found that we must get into touch with one end of this problem at a time. The question was whether we should run to Holyoke first, to Chicopee first, or to the city of Springfield first. The law requires that the location must be occupied within four years. The line from Bondsville to Springfield runs some 12 miles before we would branch off and go to Holyoke. The financial condition of the Boston and Maine became more and more involved so that it was deemed wise to make the Springfield connection first. The question raised is that Holyoke has not been served. That is the whole problem of the rearrangement of the railroad situation in Springfield. If this line to Holyoke is built – and I have no doubt but that it will be built -- the idea is to accomplish what you want us to accomplish. It was impossible, as we easily discovered, to do all of these things at a single time. Early we discovered that fact and made application to change the route to Springfield, and we had this whole matter discussed before this board and the question was decided by Mr. Hati, who was chairman at the time, that it was proper to amend our petition so as to make a location at Springfield first.

"'I am sorry that anybody should criticize the integrity of this proposition. Holyoke was loyal and earnestly urged the granting of the certificate of exigency and this railroad is not prepared to abandon any part of its program. Things with the Boston and Maine railroad which we hope will be the lessee are somewhat different now than what they had been. We have our own difficulties and have that the atmosphere will ultimately become clear and everybody will be satisfied. Springfield Homestead, Wednesday, June 25, 1913, pp1; Springfield Union, June 24, 1913; Railroad Commission Hearing for 1913.

The Aldermen of Chicopee wanted to know when the Hampden Railroad would continue its branch to Chicopee Falls. Likewise, Holyoke wanted to know about its connection. Chicopee and Holyoke would have better connections to Eastern Massachusetts if the Hampden Railroad was completed, and would not have to route traffic to Springfield, then east on Boston & Albany. Ludlow had 2 new stations slightly north of the business center of town, but no service. The State gave approvals and recommended immediate use. Mellen was no longer in leadership position of the Boston and Maine, so the new Boston and Maine Board of Directors did not consummate the Hampden Railroad lease. Brandeis had broken the Boston and Maine/New Haven monopoly by Mellen.

May 19, 1913 D. M. Wheeler, inspector, made a tour on June 18 and found the line was excellent and ready for use on Monday. The New Haven Railroad announces new Service and schedule: 12 trains daily, 4 with thru traffic from New York City to Maine, 2 local trains between Northampton and Ware. Note: 8 trains are 1100 series NH trains (100 series) from NYC/GCT-ME, 4 are 1500 series (Boston and Maine 500 series CM), locals to Northampton & Ware See -Schedule – Appendix D.

FINANCIALS OF HAMPDEN RAILROAD

On June 1, 1913 the consulting engineers report of yardage the Boston and Maine examined the work and filed a report from Arthur B Corthell to commissioners filed on July 7, 1913. The total yardage agrees with Hampden Railroad engineers report. Page 201 in the Massachusetts Railroad Commissions Report for 1913. Hampden Railroad paid Woronoco Construction Company $2,686,693.26 for work of sub-contractors of $1,090,824.07 for a mark-up of $1,595,269.19 (40%). p216 Railroad Commissioners calculated cost as $3.3M as of December 19, 1913

1913 RR commission Page 471 Hampden Railroad, Returns.
Noted under construction

Assets:

Capital Stock	$1,400,000.00
Working liabilities	2,600,000.00
Grand Total	$4,000,000.00

Liabilities:

Road and equipment	$1,629,648.74
Working assets	31,601.26
Deferred debt	2,338,750.00
Grand Total	$4,000,000.00

June 18, 1913
- Mass legislature voted down the bill providing for the lease to the Boston and Maine.
- Certificate for preliminary operation of Hampden Railroad granted. Page 198

1913 State Railroad Commission: Hampden Railroad was certified safe to use by state. But, it becomes embroiled in the interaction between of the Hampden Railroad, the New Haven and the Boston & Maine, Gillett and Mellen, as well as Brandeis crusade against Mellen.

Petition of the Hampden Railroad Corporation
for certificate preliminary to operation of its railroad.

Examination having been made of the Hampden Railroad, consisting of a single track line with sidings, extending from a connection with the Central Massachusetts branch of the Boston and Maine railroad in the town of Palmer, thence running westerly through the towns of Palmer, Belchertown, and Ludlow and the Cities of Chicopee and Springfield to a connection with the Athol branch of the Boston & Albany railroad at a point about there hundred forty feet from the junction of said branch with the main line of the Boston & Albany railroad, the total length of said Hampden railroad being about 14.81 miles – it is

Ordered, That the Board hereby certify that all laws relative to the construction of the Hampden railroad have been complied with, and that the railroad appears to be in a safe condition for operation.

Attest: CHARLES E. MANN, clerk
June 18, 1913   R. R. C. 9391

On March 31, 1913 J. P. Morgan died in Rome, Italy, only a few months after his appearance before the Pujo committee, and was buried in Hartford, Conn.
From Massachusetts Public Services report #1, 1914 for year 1913, P. 370-371 Note: this is the only certificate issued in 1913 other than the one for the Boston & Albany to relocate the Athol branch for the Hampden.
May 5,1913 Charles S. Mellen testified to Interstate Commerce Commission in Boston that he profited from stock sales and also gave money to the 1904 Republican National Campaign. In Boston Circuit Court, he also discussed the cost of road and traffic to be generated.
June 20, 1913 New Haven Railroad made a statement -- No Lease!
June 21, 1913 Hitch in opening new road! State railroad commission did not approve the lease to Boston and Maine. Hampden Railroad finished days ago and was inspected by DM Wheeler. The Railroad Commission issued a certificate of operation, but Boston and Maine says NO. Appraisals of costs are the true issue. Lease was to be for 5% of costs. The Railroad was effectively completed.
June 23.1913 there was a Public Hearing on a certificate of exigency. The route was different than originally.   Massachusetts Railroad Commission Report for 1913, pp197.
June 24,1913 Holyoke issued a complaint. Plans filed with Secretary of the

Commonwealth are not consistent with the work actually done. There were no hearings in Holyoke. The original 1910 plan was to go to Holyoke, changed to Springfield first, then the Holyoke branch after. Hampden Railroad had four years to complete the branch.

June 25, 1913 Hampden road to be probed by State Commission, plans changed from entrance to Springfield to cutoff in Ludlow to Athol Junction. No profile map with changes was filed with the Railroad Commission.

In the months afterwards, it became clear that the same man, Ralph Gillett, chaired three companies, the Hampden Railroad, The Hampden Investment Corporation, and the Woronoco Construction. Newspaper articles of the day all but accused him of a scam on the public and the investors. Charles Mellen was, of course, behind him, until the end when the construction scandals began. And behind Mellen was Morgan's money and counseling. But Mellen had problems of his own, mostly Louis Brandies.

On July 9,1913 it was reported that about thirty people from Westfield, Springfield and Ludlow toured the line on July 7th. They left the Woronoco Construction Company offices on Stebbins Street in Ludlow (Holyoke road) and went to East Springfield, then rode to Bondsville Junction. They commented the stations were well built and arranged, floors approaches and platforms were cement, Ludlow even had trees and shrubbery. The Western union telegraph lines were being installed.

On July10, 1913 New Public Service Commission begins hearings on the Hampden. The Boston and Maine could not get financing in 1911, so the Hampden Railroad was set up to build the road, Ralph Gillett covered $2,000,000 of expenses. Ralph Gillett had 4 engineers on this project for four years. Public Service Commission board questioned why the Athol branch was not used for entrance into Springfield, CS Mellen answered that the Athol Branch was a slower line.

July 17, 1913 CS Mellen "retired" from the New Haven, effective September 1, 1913.

On July 29, 1913, the Boston and Maine directors voted on agreement to operate (Massachusetts Railroad Commission 1913 pp 196) but could not formulate an agreement. And, the Boston and Maine Railroad Board of Directors reversed the previous decision and voted "Yes" to lease.

August 9, 1913 Western Union Telegraph lines are done, signal lines being installed, will take 6 more weeks. The work had not stopped.

August 19, 1913 Boston and Maine general Solicitor and Council for Hampden Railroad told Railroad Commissioners that the two corporations agreed to cost of Railroad and liability of Boston and Maine as $3.6M. Commissioners fixed capital at $3.6M

October 8. 1913 hearing began: Hampden Railroad was acting as an agent for the Boston and Maine Railroad. When Mellen became President of Boston and Maine Railroad in 1910 the Hampden Railroad project began." Boston and Maine Railroad had already reached its bond limit by Massachusetts law. This new Hampden Railroad line had to be a new corporation. Mellen made verbal agreement with Gillett, that Gillett would finance and construct the road. Boston and Maine Railroad would lease it and pay 5% of cost. (MRRC1913, pp189)

October 14, 1913: Ralph D Gillett dies from heart attack at home after a day at the Railroad Commission hearings in Boston. He traveled by train daily to Boston. See obit. – Appendix C.

December 9, 1913 Resolution to Boston and Maine Board of Directors to ratify execution of Mellen/Gillett lease, referred to the Executive Committee with report due back December 17, 1913.

December 17, 1913 Board of Directors vote that the lease was not warranted, and that the General Solicitor should communicate that to the Public Service Commission.

December 18, 1913 Copy filed to Railroad Commissioners, with a cover letter that the road was not yet completed, including the Holyoke extension.

December 29, 1913: Board of Directors of Boston and Maine voted to buy or lease the road on terms approved by the Massachusetts Railroad Commission.

January 1914, Public Service Commission report published for 1913. On page 187, we find a Petition of the Hampden Railroad for approval of an issue of bonds in the amount of $2,500,000, dated February 1, 1913, paying 5% per year. These 30 year bonds were to cover the floating debt incurred during the construction of the railroad. The bond was to be secured by a mortgage of the Railroad properties.

The response to this petition covers 32 pages in the 1913 Report. It makes very interesting reading and summarizes activities to that date. The most important points are summarized here:

This hearing was held in June 1913, and by that date, an additional expenditure of $500,000 had been incurred. The commission stated the railroad should have asked for additional funds at that time. This brings the total cost of the railroad from the original $1,400,000 to $4,400,000, an increase of $3,000,000.

The Commission describes the Road as being 14.85 miles long and includes four small stations, but no terminals or rolling stock. Therefore the entire cost of this line comes under close scrutiny, approx $290,000 per mile. This leads to an inspection of the relationship of the Hampden Railroad and the Woronoco Construction companies.

A connection from the Central Mass Railroad into Springfield was as old as that railroad itself, but no actions were taken until Mellen was in control of that line in 1910. Mr. Mellen had stated to the Commission that the Boston & Maine had reached its bond indebtedness limit, and could not afford to build this line. Mr. Mellen discussed this with Mr. Gillett, who was working on projects for the New Haven Railroad (also controlled by Mellen). After several meetings, Mellen and Gillett had made a verbal agreement for Gillett to finance and build this line, and that the Boston & Maine would lease it and pay 5% of the costs.

Gillett and others formed an association in 1910 and filed preliminary plans for the road, and filed for permits. Then he started fixing the route in each town. Meanwhile, the Boston & Maine Board of Directors authorized its president, Mr. Mellen, to make any and all arrangements for the lease of this line. By June 1911, Gillett and his associates had formed the Hampden Railroad Corporation and received a certificate of incorporation.

Mr. Gillett began negotiations with Boston & Maine on fixing the prices for excavation and overhaul and other terms and conditions of work. Boston & Maine referred the unit prices from the Chief Engineer and he inspected the proposed location and compared prices and proposed these:

Earth Cut	$ .0375 per cubic yard
Rock Cut	$1.50 per cubic yard
Ballast	$0.60 per cubic yard
Overhaul	$ .0075 per cubic yard

On June 18, 1914 the Massachusetts legislature voted down the bill providing for the lease to the Boston and Maine.

On September 2, 1914 the Hampden Railroad company filed suit against the Boston and Maine Railroad to enforce its alleged contract liability for the cost of the line, between $3,500,000 and $4,000,000.

On November 2, 1914 the Federal grand jury indicts thirty-one New Hampshire Directors, Mellen testified…

On December 2, 1914: The Hampden Railroad company filed two petitions:
- to request an extension of time for the completion of its road to Holyoke and Chicopee Falls, and
- asking that it be permitted to enter into an operating agreement with any other railroad in the Commonwealth and to sell or lease its lines to any other railroad corporation or to purchase or lease its lines to any other railroad corporation. These requests were granted by the Massachusetts Legislature. These extensions must be completed by July 1, 1918

June 5, 1918, Springfield Union:

"Mellen Says Separation of New Haven and Boston and Maine Spoiled Scheme

Charles S. Mellen, former president of the New Haven and Boston and Maine systems, walked into the trial of the suit of the Hampden Railroad Corporation against the Boston and Maine Corporation to recover an alleged construction account of $4,800,000, in the Superior Court before Chief Justice John A. Aiken yesterday and took the entire responsibility for the Boston and Maine connection with the Hampden work on his own shoulders. Throughout his testimony of the morning former president Mellen emphasized the responsibility of himself and the Boston and Maine in the construction of the Hampden railroad, detailing his plans as to the lease of the Hampden road and his purpose while president and director of the Boston and Maine railroad to make no move without the knowledge of the directors, it's stockholders being kept fully informed. Mr. Mellen made it clear during his connection with the Boston and Maine; he represented also the New Haven interests, which had control of the Boston and Maine through a holding company.

The direct examination of Mr. Mellen ended shortly after 2 o'clock yesterday afternoon and Atty. George L. Mayberry of the Boston and Maine railroad's council took the railroad magnate in hand for cross-examination. It was during this proceeding that a mild sensation was sprung on the presentation of a letter alleged to have been written by Charles S. Mellen to C. W. Crooker, on of the council for the Boston and Maine railroad in the present trial, October 1918, the court permitted the following extract to be introduced in evidence:

"The Hampden Railroad was all right in it's inception and would have proved a valuable property and had the connections then existing on the New Haven been allowed to continue, but when the properties were separated, then it became of little or no value to the Maine, which has assumed the obligations in connection with the same as the only connecting line that could either lease or own the same under Massachusetts laws."

"The Boston and Maine should relieve itself of the Hampden burden if it can: or not as a legal proposition which as I am a layman I cannot answer. If I may so express myself I should regard it as a duty to Maine security holders to avoid by all means the Hampden burden upon the Boston and Maine under present conditions."

"Indeed there is a question in my mind if in the equity of the New Haven should in the inception of that enterprise have become a party to the obligations assumed, it having been in reality a scheme for the benefit of the two properties, the Maine assuming all the burden because it was the directly connecting line and could legally do so, but it never would have done so but for New Haven control."

Soon after Mr. Mellen said soon after he became president of the Boston and Maine railroad the development of the Massachusetts Central arose, but the strong interest of the New Haven road in the projects whereby the Central might be improved cooled. Mr. Mellen declared that the proposed extension of the Central from Bondsville, the Hampden road, was not planned or built as a competing line: by this line it was proposed to divert travel from one line to another with the better equipped for this sort of patronage. In response to a question by Atty. Dodge, Mr. Mellen said that a tunnel connecting the Boston stations, for the convenience of travel, a service foremost always in the minds of railroad men, was preferable to the proposed extension by way of Bondsville.

Mr. Mellen recalled having conversation with Ralph D Gillett, relative to the proposed extension, but the financial condition of the Boston and Maine railroad at the time prohibited financing the project. Mr. Gillett was able to finance the plans, hence, Mr. Mellen favorably considered his ideas. The Massachusetts Central had been a losing proposition, as the witness recalled, and it was incumbent upon those concerned to cause a change. He knew of propositions considering lines to Chicopee, to Springfield, and to Holyoke.

Mr. Mellen was asked by Mr. Dodge if he initiated the Hampden railroad project, or who did if he didn't. "I did," said Mr. Mellen. "I always take it on my shoulders that which I cannot put on the shoulders of anybody else."

Mr. Mellen emphasized his statement that the directors of the Boston & Maine always knew what he was about and in this connection he declared that the directors talked with him about the proposed line to

Athol Junction and Chicopee, both plans contemplating junction with the New Haven system. The most convenient and less costly was the one finally determined upon. Its operating advantages were equal to any possible line which could be designed.

Continuing under the examination of Atty. Dodge, former President Mellen said that the Hampden railroad was ready for operation by the Boston & Maine railroad in mid-1913; money was being expended deliberately in preparation for through service. The lease, which figures so largely in the present suit of the Hampden corporation against the Boston & Maine, was signed, Mr. Mellen testified, in the summer of 1913, and according to his best opinion the fact was communicated to the directors of the Boston & Maine.

The direct examination by Atty. Dodge was continued immediately after the resumption of court after the noon recess. Mr. Mellen, in response to Atty. Dodge, placed the value of the Hampden railroad property with the lease at $3,020,000, the salvage being what he estimated it previously during his testimony, as just old junk.

The entire Hampden Railroad enterprise was more costly then originally estimated, Mr. Mellen stated, the first figures as to cost being $2,100,000, but Mr. Mellen said that he hoped at the same time it would be less. "The Hampden railroad was handled in a way that cost more than I wished for," said Mr. Mellen. "I made no complaint, but I was sorry the road was so expensive. I thought it was made unduly expensive by the requirements of the Boston & Maine engineering department."

Former-president Mellen denied that it was part of any plan to parallel the Boston & Maine railroad by building a branch road from Chicopee or Holyoke. "It was never the intention to build to Holyoke to through Chicopee to Springfield," declared Mr. Mellen. Neither branch, as proposed, was a part of the Boston & Maine enterprise. The cost of the branch by way of Chicopee was estimated at $2,800,000. As to using the Boston & Albany tracks Mr. Mellen believed the plan impracticable. It was stated by Mr. Mellen that after certain traffic contracts had been made between the New Haven and the New York Central railroad interest in the lagged." Springfield Union, June 5, 1918

June 6, 1918: During the court case, Oren E Parks, Purchasing Supervisor for Hampden Railroad, claims he consulted and had approval from Arthur B Corthell, Boston and Maine Engineering Dept, on the specifications.

In 1913, Parks placed salvage value of the road at $120,000.

$50,000	Rails
$12,500	Ties
$ 8,250	Fasteners, frogs, switches
$35,400	Bridges
$ 1,000	Water Tank
$ 2,400	60 acres at $50/acre, and misc. materials

June 19, 1918: A verdict in favor of the Boston and Maine was ordered in Superior Court at Springfield, Mass. Case appealed to State Supreme Court.

February 1921: Mass State Senate passed a bill extending the time, until July 1, 1921, that the branch lines to Chicopee and Holyoke must be completed and placed in operation.

March 17, 1921: William E. Gilbert was appointed receiver for the Hampden Railroad Corporation by Superior Court, as a result of a suit filed by Hampden Bank, Westfield, Mass.

June 3, 1926: Auction of all properties. Bids opened within 10 days, on June `14, Salvage awarded to for $29,000 to Mark Angel from Roxbury Scrap Iron Co. Angel purchased all fixed and removable assets, rail, ties, stations, bridges.

June 15, 1926: Right of Way sold to the Montague company, a subsidiary of the Turners Falls Power and Electric Company. It was a real estate investment.

1948: Town of Palmer opens a landfill operation in the Palmer Cut, west of State St. This operation was closed in 1971 when the cut was filled.

In the 1940's, numerous changes were made to the abutments to allow for wider roads for increased automobile traffic in Chicopee and Ludlow. Many were removed altogether.

The Hampden was also considered for a freight road to deliver materials for the new Westover Field airbase built in the 1940's.

CHAPTER ELEVEN

THE INDUSTRIAL CONNECTION

There was no direct industrial connection or backing in the Hampden Railroad but there was a lot of hope and interest. The Western New England Magazine in 1913 believed that it would bring about important changes in the industrial life of Western New England by giving to it greatly improved railroad facilities in the form of a new line to Boston that is shorter than the Boston & Albany and one whose grades are much lower…It is, in part, the beginning of a feasible plan to bring back to New England the business which has been diverted to southern ports because of the congestion existing on lines feeding western business to New England. They also believed that there were possibilities of business accruing from the West, the Northwest and the Great Lakes into Western Massachusetts.

In Springfield there was high interest during construction. Hartford Tubing talked about establishing a factory in 1912. Puncture Proof Tire purchased twenty acres of land near Wood Pond in Ludlow in 1912.

Stevens-Duryea Company on Highland Terrace was to be serviced by the Hampden. This building is on the corner of Page Blvd and Stevens St. In June 1981, I spoke with an old-timer at Jahn Foundry and he related that this 1912 Stevens-Duryea Company plant was closed on December 4, 1926. This entire industrial area was eventually served by Boston & Albany's Athol Branch. Most of this area was a Westinghouse facility in the 1920's, and the Stevens Duryea building was used by Westinghouse Electric and then AlaVel Industries until it closed in the late 1980's. All the Westinghouse buildings were demolished in 2013 for a proposed casino.

Photo 1147: station 15. Finished track in East Springfield in 1913 this area is still heavily wooded and rural. Today, this entire area is heavily industrialized. Author's collection

JUNCTIONS:
ATHOL JUNCTION WITH BOSTON AND ALBANY

Tower and Mainline Signals at Athol Junction 1912, Author's collection

Track work at Junction and signals, reverse view from above, note signal box by telegraph pole in both views. Author's collection

Hampden Junction with Central Mass line of Boston & Maine

Photos 715 and 1199: Hampden junction area being prepared for connection to Central Mass branch of Boston & Maine railroad, July and November 1912. Author's collection

CHAPTER TWELVE

STORIES I'VE BEEN TOLD

Ray Mermot from Longmeadow wrote a 1972 rebuttal article in the Springfield newspaper concerning the newspaper article from July 23rd 1959 about Patrick J. Glocester who claimed to be an engineer for the Hampden Railroad. He kept the engine ready at the engine house for 46 years just in case it was needed to view the railroad. 1913-1959, a period of 46 years. I find this interesting, because the Hampden didn't have an engine house or an engine, this must have been a Boston & Maine position. There was no further newspaper coverage of this story.

Bob Elfenstone: he and some companions rode a railroad truck or work car on the Hampden as a youngster. The boys pushed the truck uphill to Three Rivers, then as it started to roll west, they all jumped on, and "shot thru Ludlow", across Bircham Bend trestle, finally stopping in East Springfield. He boys spent the rest of the day walking to Ludlow since they needed to get home, and did not want to be found out. This story could not be told while Bob was alive, he was afraid his wife would find out. This was before 1935. This story was related to me by Bob Buck.

David Swirk, whose family owns land by Hampden Railroad / Boston & Maine junction, the family's land has an artesian well from this time. A mile marker is on the property, not easily accessible. David tells the family's story from the construction days: A construction or railroad foreman or someone in authority came to the farmhouse to ask for water, when he tasted the water from the family well, he said "this water is not fit for my horse" and left. Later, a crew from the construction showed up with a steam drill and drilled them a new well. This well is still on the property today. The photo on the following page is likely the same well digger.

Well digging at Sullivan's Place. 6/29/1912, station 890. Author's collection

CHAPTER THIRTEEN

EPILOGUE or EPITAPH

More from 1913 Public Service Commission
Hampden Railroad

"The Hampden railroad was completed some months ago between Bondsville and Athol Junction, but has not yet been put into operation. Neither has the branch line to Holyoke nor the connection with Chicopee Falls as specified in the charter of the road have been built. Questions have been raised as to the validity of the present location of the Hampden railroad and the obligation of the corporation to build the branch line to Holyoke and the Chicopee Falls connection in addition to the road which has already been built.

With reference to this the Commission in its report on the petition of the Hampden road for right to issue bonds said:

It seems clear that neither the Hampden Railroad Corporation nor the Boston & Maine Railroad is now in a financial position to build the branch line into Chicopee to connect with the Chicopee Falls branch of the Boston & Maine railroad or the branch line into Holyoke. Indeed it is doubtful whether a legal location for these branch lines could now be obtained. If under the terms of its charter the Hampden Railroad Corporation is under obligation to build these branch lines within four years from the date of its certificate of incorporation under penalty of forfeiture of its charter, it seems desirable that the two railroad companies should join in a petition to the Legislature for relief of that obligation.

The directors of the Boston & Maine Railroad have recently expressed their unwillingness to ratify the lease of the Hampden railroad at the present time, stating as one of the reasons for such unwillingness the fact that the branch line to Holyoke has not yet been constructed. We believe that it is in the public interest that the road having been constructed, should be put into operation as soon as possible, and to that end that appropriate legislation should be had settling the exact status of the road as constructed, determining whether the lines to Chicopee and Holyoke should be constructed or not, and providing upon what terms and conditions, if any, the Boston & Maine Railroad may operate or acquire the road as constructed."

From Massachusetts Public Services report #1, 1914 for year 1913, General Discussion P. 101-102

The Committee recommended the railroad be used right away, also the Hampden Railroad and Boston & Maine should petition the Legislature for release of the obligation to build two branch lines to Chicopee and Holyoke.

Philip E. Johnson

CHAPTER FOURTEEN

A TRIP ON THE HAMPDEN TODAY-2013

Remnants, Monuments, Tombstones

- **Cement abutments/monoliths** in Palmer cross many streets and Swift River
- **Mile markers**, stones indicating mileage from Boston, I have located 4, but 5 more may still exist
- **Straight section** of eastbound lane of the Mass Pike (Route 90) from Exit 6 to a point just east of the Ludlow plaza.
- **Abutments** in Chicopee River and on both shores by Bircham Bend.
- **Concrete footings, and fence posts** could be found in the deep woods.
- **Station foundation** at Three Rivers station
- **Culverts**, Fuller Brook by Shawinigan Dr Chicopee, by Tower Rd, Ludlow.
- **Deep cuts** in Ludlow (Minnechaug mountain), Belchertown, and Palmer
- **Station Paving stones** used as an embankment in front of a home on Railroad St-Three Rivers, MA.

There is a **monument** (tombstone) by the west abutment on Palmer Street, placed by the Palmer Historical Commission and the Massachusetts Electric Company.

Fence posts: visible along cut near old Palmer dump on Summer Street also some in woods by Shawinigan Drive, Chicopee. The author noted 5 posts standing along edge of road opposite houses at the Ludlow end until the road was moved to align with West Avenue. The fence line goes Southwest along Monsanto property line.

May 1983, concrete posts by Miller Street, Ludlow.

June 20, 1983, no posts seen along Mass turnpike between exits 6 to 8

Please note: most, if not all, of the roadbed has been purchased or has reverted to the original owners. You may be trespassing if you attempt to hike the property without permission.

Author's note: The Hampden was planned for double track main line. The construction plans filed with the cities showed the constructed track to be off-center to the south, as if there would be another track north of the center-line.

Newspapers report the line is graded for double, Author does not find any evidence of 2-track main, cuts and fills were not wide enough for that. All cement work that is still visible and bridge abutments are too narrow for two tracks. The Bircham Bend trestle and the Swift River bridge would be very expensive to add a second track, Bircham Bend is 1100 feet long, and used over 1400 tons of steel as well as the river work for footings, and Swift River crossing is over 700 feet. None of the construction photos show enough extra width for two tracks.

Legacy: mythical status among Western Mass railfans, as well as many Palmer residents.

Appendix A --Hampden Expenses

Item	Cost
Earth Cuts: 987,836 cubic yards at 37.5	$370,438.47
Rock Cuts:1,104,796 cubic yards at 1.50	$1,657,194.00
Overhaul: 87,794,779 cubic yards at .0034	$658,460.79
Bridge Station 38 (Page Blvd)	$82,330.50
Shoring Boston and Maine track at Whitings	$255.00
Misc. wooden highway bridges and highway fences	$3,216.86
Rip-rap, woods pond	$1,435.84
Clearing, grubbing	$5,061.37
Track and top ditches	$2,491.63
Changing location, Athol Branch	$5,178.88
E. Springfield passing track	$1,414.83
Changes in road, E Spr station	$2,073.24
Changes in road, Ludlow station	$3,549.20
Widening fill	$1,252.32
Track changes, Athol Jct.	$6,007.77
Boston and Maine track, Bondsville	$35.75
Highway change, Minnechaug Mt.	$10,412.31
Highway change, Butler Rd	$11,399.35
Highway change, Robbins Rd	$2,860.71
Highway change, Station 97	$1,185.16
Highway change, Fuller Rd	$10,351.02
Highway change, Station 181	$195.00
Highway change, Station 241	$7,979.80
Highway change, Station 247	$6,864.62
Relay Springfield water pipe	$12,135.79
Highway change, Station 310	$868.00
Highway change, Station 395	$400.36
Highway change, Parkers' Rd	$5,623.62
Highway change, Wood's Rd	$1,401.01
Highway change, station 681	$627.23
Highway change, Graveline's rd	$17,663.15
Highway change, station 768	$387.47
Highway change, station 784	$2,409.85
Highway change, station 838	$631.63
Highway change, Bigda's rd	$5,032.56
Highway change, station 891	$614.18
Highway change, station 893	$6,121.36
Highway change, station 904	$6,042.93
Highway change, Courtemanile Place	$164.92
Highway change, station 815	$10,702.03
Fuller St drainage	$226.09

Appendix A --Hampden Expenses (cont)

Item	Cost
Right of Way	$152,399.19
Bridges, trestles, & Culverts	$413,252.34
Ties	$72,837.59
Rails	$91,429.99
Frogs and Switches	$1,412.45
Track Fastenings and other material	$18,484.45
Ballast	$49,657.73
Track Laying and surfacing	$113,914.60
Fencing right of way	$19,254.88
crossings and signs	$199.62
Interlocking signal and other apparatus	$112.47
Station building and fixtures	$41,223.41
Water Stations	$2,300.68
Rent of equipment	$2,247.42
Injuries to persons	$110.31
Law expenses	$1,211.74
Stationary & printing	$698.53
Insurance	$10,015.49
Taxes	$1,277.41
Release for claim of damages Charles A. Rich	$455.37
Release for claim of damages William Blackmar	$330.00
other expenditures	$11,637.17
Interest and commissions	$102,924.55
Engineering	$46,595.00
Law expenses	$11,795.00
Total	**$4,088,473.99**
MAY 1913	
Newspaper Total	$4,145,683.04
Difference	**($57,209.05)**

Springfield News, June 27, 1913

APPENDIX B – STATION NUMBERS

Station	Location	Town	Milepost	Location
0	Athol Junction	Springfield	95	Athol Junction
30.40	Butler rd	Springfield		
	E Springfield Station-Rose St	Springfield	94	East Springfield Station
36	Page Blvd	Springfield		
60.67	Robbins Road	Springfield		
83	Bircham Bend Trestle	Springfield	93	South abutment Bircham Bend Bridge-MP found
86.56	E. Main St & trolley	Chicopee		
97.04	Fuller rd	Chicopee		
111	Jnct with Chicopee Falls Br.	Chicopee		Branch never built
113	Fuller Brook	Chicopee	92	on turnpike, east of Fuller Brook
141.25	New Fuller Rd	Chicopee	91	on turnpike, west of Fuller Road
180.8	West St-Fuller St	Ludlow	90	on turnpike
240.105	Davis St	Ludlow		
	Chicopee Falls Rd	Ludlow		North or Holyoke Rd
	Mero St	Ludlow		
247.26	Fuller St	Ludlow		
258.69	Ludlow Center Rd	Ludlow	89	on turnpike, at Wood Pond
(moved)	Sewall St	Ludlow		
310.27	Chapin St	Ludlow	88	on turnpike
354.6	East St	Ludlow		
370.22	Miller St	Ludlow		
None	Tower Rd	Ludlow		(new road)
396.45	Minnechaug Mt (west)	Ludlow	87	West of Minnechaug mtn cut
459.24	Moore St	Ludlow		
670.43	Alden St	Ludlow		
679.26	Broad Br	Palmer	86	In Minnechaug mtn cut-found
681.29	Paine-Private Rd	Palmer	85	
699.54	South St	Palmer	84	Btw South St and Palmer Cut
768.2	So Liberty St	Palmer	83	At South Liberty St
777.98	Athol Br, Boston & Albany	Palmer		
784.12	North St/Railroad St	Palmer		
791.6	Central Vermont rr	Palmer		
793.54	Swift River	Palmer		
833.59	Route 181, trolley	Palmer	82	Btw Swift Rv and Palmer St on high fill-MP found

Station	Location	Town	Milepost	Location
847.32	Palmer St	Palmer		
None	Pleasant St	Palmer	81	In cut, west of Boston and Maine bridge MP found
893.53	Central Mass Bridge	Palmer		
903.76	Bondsville highway	Palmer		
914.81	Road to Hastings crossing	Palmer		
923.78	Junction Central Mass	Palmer	80	near Boston and Maine Junction at Forest Lake

APPENDIX C—OBITUARY OF RALPH D. GILLETT

Sudden Death of Ralph D. Gillett
Hampden Railroad President is Victim of Angina Pectoris
Fire Causes Attack
Western Massachusetts Construction Wizard; Native of Westfield.

Westfield, Oct 14 (1913) Ralph Dickenson Gillett, aged 47, president of the Hampden railroad, and one of the leading men in the business life of Western Massachusetts, died suddenly at his home in Tekoa terrace at 8:30 o'clock tonight. Death was due to an attack of angina pectoris brought on by excitement over a slight fire in the basement of the household.

Mr. Gillett and Atty. Henry W. Ely had been to Boston today. They returned on the 7:40 o'clock train this evening and Mr. Gillett appeared to be in good health. He went home at once in his auto. When he arrived there, the family was more of less excited by a fire in the partitions in the basement. Mr. Gillett also became alarmed. Shortly afterward he became ill and death came within a few minutes. Dr. J. B. Atwater was summoned, but nothing could be done for the victim of the attack.

Mr. Gillett, through the construction of the Hampden railroad, established a reputation as a railroad builder of exceptional daring and ability, and was apparently launching upon a course that would make him a figure of national importance in solving intricate problems of New England transportation. His record in construction and in finance had been one of the remarkable successes and his interest in various enterprises in this section of the state marked him as a man of broad understanding of the business opportunities and hopes of the state.

Mr. Gillett was born in Westfield Nov. 28, 1865, the son of Darwin L. and Sarah Dickenson Gillett. He was graduated from the Westfield high school in 1883. he became associated with his father in the dry goods business, the firm first being called D. L. Gillett & Co., and later D. L. Gillett & Co Son. He was manager of the establishment for some time. The building in which it was housed was destroyed by fire, the latter part in 1896. Mr. Gillett cleared out the ruins and built the present block, also constructing about the same time the beautiful residence for the family in Tekoa Terrace.

Early in the '90s of the last century Mr. Gillett became interested in transportation, confining his attention chiefly to street railways. He was active in the formation of the Woronoco Street Railway company. In 1893 he promoted and built the Highland Street railway extending from Mill Street to Woronoco Park. He owned the park and proceeded to develop it after he had established a means of communication with the town. He remained at the head of affairs when the Woronoco Company and the Highland line amalgamated, and until the amalgamated system was absorbed by the Springfield street railway.

One of his biggest street railway contracts was the building of the extensive Berkshire street railway system, which was constructed in 1900. He also built the line from Westfield to Huntington for the Western Massachusetts Street Railway Company. He was a close friend of former-president Mellen of the New Haven road. As owner of the Woronoco Construction Company, he carried out large contracts for the New Haven system. He was one of the promoters and president of the Buffalo, Rochester, and Eastern railroad. He was also an officer of the Western Massachusetts Construction Company, owner of the Peck Manufacturing Company of Pittsfield, and in other business projects in the Berkshires.

Mr. Gillett took a keen interest in civic affairs of his town and state, and in the political life of the state and nation. He was an alternate delegate for the Republican national convention in 1908.

Horses always owned a warm spot in the corner of his heart. As a young man, he was more or less interested in stock raising for a time, and was an ardent sportsman during the heyday of racing at Woronoco Park. His genial nature and humor made his comradeship much sought. His acquaintances were many who knew him as a good comrade as well as an exceptionally powerful business man.
He was a member of the Westfield club, and an attendant at the First Congregational church. When he erected his new residence in Tekoa Terrace, he turned over his old residence on Broad Street for use as an old people's home. This was done in honor of his mother and the institution was named "the Sarah Gillett home".

Mr. Gillett leaves his widow, who was Miss Anne Sherman before her marriage: three sons, Edgar L., Darwin L., and Ralph of Westfield; three daughters, Mrs. Charles Tift of Springfield, and Anne and Elizabeth of Westfield.

Springfield newspaper morning edition, Wednesday, October 15, 1913.

■■

Many pay tribute to Ralph Gillett
Business houses in Westfield are closed during funeral
C.S.Mellen Present
Former Head of New Haven close friend of popular young man
Westfield, October 17 (1913)

With a gentle secession of all business in Westfield during the funeral hours, the services over the body of Ralph D. Gillett were held this afternoon in the home in Tekoa terrace and were largely attended by the friends, business acquaintances and the townspeople. Promptly at 3 o'clock all of the stores and business houses in Elm Street were closed and did not open until the hour had passed.

There was no traffic on the street railway lines during the first five minutes of the hour and the crews of the cars bowed their heads in respect to the memory of Mr. Gillett. The flag on the liberty pole in Park Square was at half-staff during the day. The police officers of the town also stood with heads uncovered during the five minutes that the street railway paid tribute to Mr. Gilllett.

■■

Delegations of business men from Pittsfield, Springfield, and Holyoke were present and among the mourners was Charles S. Mellen, former president of the New Haven road and a close friend of Mr. Gillett. There was a profusion of floral offerings and the family has been the recipients of many letters and telegrams of condolences from the friends of Mr. Gillett. The services were simple but impressive. Rev. H. M. Dyckman, pastor of First Congregational Church and Rev. John H. Lockwood of Springfield, pastor emeritus of the church were in charge. The active bearers were James R. Savery of Pittsfield, H. J. Bradley of Pittsfield, G. E Mitchell, Oren E. Parks, Charles F. Ensworth and Archie D. Robinson, all of this town. The honorary bearers were Henry W. Ely, Charles J. Little, and Edward T. Fowler of this town, A. W. Eaton of Pittsfield, J. H. and William Skinner of Holyoke, H. W. Bowman and Albert Steiger of Springfield. The burial was in Pine Hill cemetery.

Appendix D -- Recreated Spring 1913 Train Schedule

Eastbound NYC to Boston					June 1, 1913	
	114	**1524**	**1528**	**110**	**1564**	**1566**
	Express	Local	Local	Express	Local	Local
NYC-GCT	11:33 PM	NH RR		10:50 AM	NH RR	
New Haven	1:43 AM			12:43 PM		
Springfield	3:35 AM			2:08 PM		
Springfield lv.	3:25 AM	Boston & Albany Train 1114	7:30 AM	9:00 AM	2:12 PM	Boston & Albany Train 1110	5:05 PM	5:35 PM
Athol Jct	3:31 AM		7:36 AM	9:06 AM	2:18 PM		5:11 PM	5:41 PM
Barre	4:47 AM	Boston and Maine RR			3:11 PM	Boston and Maine RR		
Boston	6:40 AM				4:57 PM			

Westbound Boston to NYC					June 1, 1913	
	113	**1501**	**1517**	**109**	**1529**	**1545**
	Express	Local	Local	Express	Local	Local
Boston	11:35 PM	Boston and Maine RR		11:00 AM	Boston and Maine RR	
Waltham	11:57 PM			11:18 AM		
Barre	1:40 AM			12:50 PM		
Athol Jct	2:40 AM	Boston & Albany Train 1113	7:20 AM	11:25 AM	1:40 PM	Boston & Albany Train 1109	3:40 PM	7:35 PM
Springfield ar.	2:45 AM		7:25 AM	11:30 AM	1:45 PM		3:45 PM	7:40 PM
Springfield lv.	2:50 AM	NH RR			1:50 PM	NH RR		
New Haven	4:35 AM				3:10 PM			
NYC-GCT	6:57 AM				5:03 PM			

Sources:
David Rooney collection
Leroy Beaujon collection
Philip Johnson

Boston & Albany 6/22/1913 + supplement #1

NH Lines West 6/1/1913, 6/23/1913

Boston and Maine southern Division and Central Mass Local 6/23/1913
Springfield Newspaper June 2, 1913, June 19, 1913

INDEX

Name	Page	Name	Page
Angel, Mark	93	Holbrook	31
Angelo, Calasantis	35	Horn, H. T.	79
Atwater, J. B	109	Johnson, Esther	iii
Austin, Mark	i	Johnson, William	39
Birnie, Judge	35	Kurrie, H. D. O.	84
Blakeslee, Clarence W.	7, 17, 54	Lafferty, A. N.	7, 39
Bowie, Frank E	34	Lawrence, William F.	83
Bowler, Madeline	i, 24, 36, 55, 58	Ley, Fred T.	7
Bowman, Henry	6, 110	Little, Charles J.	110
Bradley, H.J.	110	Lockwood, Rev. John H.	110
Brandeis, Louis	85, 87	Lowenthal, Larry	i, 1
Buck, Robert	i, 56	MacLeod	84
Buckwheat, Frank	18	MacNayr, Lloyd	i
Cabot	31	Mann, Charles E.	7, 13, 14, 87
Consedine, Chief	35	Mayberry, George L.	91
Corthell, Arthur B.	11	McDonald, John	7
Crane, A.S.	79	McGerra, Edward	34
Crimmons, Timothy J.	38	McHenry, E. H.	13, 15
Dodge, Atty.	91	McLaller, Archibald	34
		Mellen, Charles S.	4, 5, 8, 11, 13, 14, 15, 80, 81, 82, 83, 85, 87, 88, 89, 90, 91, 92,
Durkee, Henry S.	7, 10, 17, 19		
Dyckman, Rev. H. M.	110	Mermot, Ray	103
Eaton, Arthur W.	6, 110	Mitchell, G. E.	110
Elfenstone, Bob	99	Mocci, Maria	35
Ely, Henry W.	6, 7, 12, 84, 85, 110,	Morgan, J. P.	2, 5, 8, 15, 87, 88
Ensworth, Charles F.	110	Mosley, F.S.	54
Ford, George	56	Nimke, Robert W.	4
Ford, Henry	3	Nobel, Alfred	3
Ford, W. H.	79, 81	Noret, Tony	65
Forristell, A.D.	79	O'Connor, Thomas J.	84
Fowler, Edward T.	110	Opielowski, Phil	i
		Parks, Oren E.	6, 10, 11, 81, 93, 110
Fuller, Charles	i, 36, 55, 58		
Gilbert, William E.	93	Pollock, B. R.	79
Gillett, Anne	110	Querino, Solli	37
Gillett, Darwin L.	109, 110	Ray, W. F.	79
Gillett, Edgar L	6, 110	Rollins	31
Gillett, Elizabeth	110	Robinson, Archie D.	6, 7, 110
Gillett, Ralph	110	Ryan, William	7
Gillett, Ralph D.	2, 4, 5, 6, 7, 8, 13, 14, 15, 16, 17, 18, 82, 83, 87, 88, 89, 90, 92, 109, 110		
Gillett, Sarah Dickenson	109	Savery, James R.	110
Glocester, Patrick J.	99	Sherman, Anne	110
Gloste, Patrick J.	35	Skinner, J. H.	110
Greene, J. R.	27	Skinner, Joseph A.	6
		Skinner, William	110
		Smith	22
		Steiger, Albert	110
		Swirk, David	99

Name	Page
Tift, Mrs. Charles	110
Trelehler, Dr.	35
Walsh, James	34
Wheeler, D. M.	81, 86
White, Mayor of Holyoke	84
Wiggiris, C.H.	79
Wroe, Lewis	53, 56, 65

Works Cited

[1]*Springfield Homestead*, Saturday, 2 March 1911, pp 2, Print

[2]43rd Annual Report of Railroad Commissioners 1912 for year 1911, pp 228, 229 Print

[3]*Springfield Republican, 21* May 1912

[4]*Springfield Republican*, 28 May 1911

[5]Kirkman, Marshall M. *Building and Repairing Railways. Supplement to the Science of Railways.* New York: World Railway Pub., 1904. 47. Print.

[6]"Dynamite Drills." *Springfield Homestead* 2 Mar. 1911: n. pag. Print

[7]Railroad DeLuxe Is Title Given Hampden Railroad." *Springfield Homestead* 3 Jan. 1914: n. pag. Print.

[8]Barnes, Fred Asa, M.C.E. "Steel Trestles." *Railroad Construction.* By Charles Lee Crandall, M.C.E. 1st ed. New York: McGraw-Hill Book, 1913. 229-30. Print. 4th Impression.

[9]"Hitch in Railroad Plans.", *The Springfield Daily Republican*, 19 June 1913: 5. Print.

OTHER REFERENCE MATERIALS USED

"Big Cuts and Fills to Be Made." *Springfield Daily Republican*, 8 Dec. 1911, Daily ed.: n. pag. Print.

"Bullets Cause Death." *Palmer Journal*, 14 Feb. 1913, Volume LXIII ed.: n. pag. Print.

"Cutting Across Hampden County with Modern Railroad.", *Springfield Union*, [Springfield, MA] 13 Jan. 1912: n. pag. Print.

"Diversified Operations Take Place on Hampden Railroad.", *Springfield Republican*, 2 June 1912: n. pag. Print.

"Hampden Railroad To Be Probed By The State Commission",*Springfield Homestead*, 25 June 1913 pp1, Wednesday ed.: n. pag. Print.

"Head Pounded with Rock.", *Palmer Journal*, 27 Dec. 1912: n. pag. Print.

"Local Intelligence -work on the Hampden Road., *Springfield Daily Republican*, 8 Dec.

1911, Daily ed.: n. pag. Print.

"Ludlow.", *Springfield Republican*, [Springfield, MA] 21 May 1912: n. pag. Print.

"Ludlow.", *The Springfield Republican*, 05 June 1913: 14., *The Springfield Republican*. Historical Archives. Web.

"Man Killed by Fall.", *Palmer Journal*, 21 June 1912: n. pag. Print.

"Mayor Fletcher of Chicopee Tells of Conversation Regarding the Hampden Railroad Route.", *Springfield Republican,* 28 May 1911: n. pag. Print.

"Mellen Indicted for Hampden Deal." *New York Times,* 30 June 1914, Boston ed.: n. pag. Print.

"Petition Opposed.", *Springfield Union,* 24 June 1913, pp1: n. pag. Print.

"Railroad Construction" *The Elements of Railroad Engineering: Prepared for the Students of the International Correspondence Schools, Scranton, Pa.,* 1st ed. Vol. II. Scranton: Colliery Engineer, 1897. 997-99. Print.

"*Springfield Union.* 19 June 1912: n. pag. Print.

"Thorndike Had Leg Amputated." *Palmer Journal,* 2 Aug. 1912: n. pag. Print.

"Warm Hearing on Extension Plans.", *Springfield Union,* 18 Apr. 1914: n. pag. Print.

Continued Hearing on Request for Additional Bond Issue. Holyoke Complaint - Atty. Ely Explains the Situation Replying to Paper City's Solicitor

Dynamite Drills.", *Springfield Homestead*, [Springfield, MA] 2 Mar. 1911: n. pag. Print.

En.wikpedia.org/wiki/Charles Sanger Mellen. Digital image., *Wikpedia the Free Encyclopedia.* Wikmedia Foundation, Inc., 24 Mar. 2013. Web. 02 Apr. 2013.

Jennings, William P. "The Hampden Railroad", *Western New England Magazine*, III.2 (1913): 8-11. Abstract. *B&M Bulletin,* (1972): n. pag. Print.

Lindstrom, Diane, B.A.,M.A., Ph.D. "Microsoft Encarta Encyclopedia 2005 : 22 Results Lindstrom, Diane, B.A., M.A., Ph.D., *Morgan, John Pierpont.* Digital image, *Http://encarta.msn.com©.* Microsoft® Encarta© Online Encyclopedia 2005, 2005. Web. 24 Jan. 2005.

Mann, Charles E., Clerk, comp. "Railroad Locations -- Orders." *43rd Annual Report of the Railroad Commissioners for the Year 1911. Hampden Railroad vs. City of Chicopee.* Vol. 43. Massachusetts: Commonwealth of, 1911. 227-28. Print.

Mann, Charles E., Clerk. "Appendix - Orders. *43rd Annual Report of the Railroad Commissioners for the Year 1911.* Vol. 1911. Massachusetts: Commonwealth of, 1911. 228-29. Print.

Mann, Charles E., Clerk. "Appendix Orders -- Railroad Locations.",*43rd Annual Report of the Railroad Commissioners for the Year 1911.* Vol. 43. Massachusetts: Commonwealth of, n.d. 28. Print.

Petition of the Hampden Railroad Corporation for certificate under the provisions of section 71, part II, chapter 463, Acts of 1906, preliminary to construction. - approved

Petition of the Hampden Railroad Corporation that the Board fix the route of its railroad in the City of Chicopee.

*The Elements of Railroad Engineering: Prepared for the Students of the International Correspondence Schools, Scranton, Pa.,*1st ed. Vol. II. Scranton: Colliery Engineer, 1897. 997-99. Print.

Western New England Magazine, III.2 (1913): n. pag. Abstract, .*B & M Bulletin,* II.2 (1972): 11. Print.

White, MacLeod Bishop, Stone. " Appendix -Orders, Capital Stocks and Bonds.", *First Annual Report of the Public Service Commission and the Forty-fifth Annual Report of the Board of Railroad Commissioners.* Vol. 1913. Boston: Wright & Potter Printing, State Printers, 1914. 191. Print. 45th Railroad Commission.

White, MacLeod Bishop, Stone. " Appendix -Orders, Capital Stocks and Bonds." First Annual Report of the Public Service Commission and the Forty-fifth Annual Report of the Board of Railroad Commissioners. Vol. 1st Public Service. Massachusetts: Commonwealth Of, N.d. 192. Print. 45th Railroad Commission.

ABOUT THE AUTHOR, PHILIP E. JOHNSON

Growing up in Springfield, Massachusetts during the 50's and 60's, I remember seeing the trains crossing in Winchester Square and by Watershops Pond, and even across Five Mile pond when swimming with my family. Beginning with model trains and riding on tourist trains as a child, I have always loved trains. When I was in my early 20's, I had a job where I was a field service engineer in eastern Hampden County. This gave me ample opportunity to view many branch lines in operation and investigate active and abandoned railroad lines. I became a member of Amherst Railroad Society as a young adult where I have remained a member for 40 years. As an engineer, I enjoy researching the history of random lines and can usually spot where a railroad once ran based on the slope of the terrain. Our family vacations many times had a railroad theme at least one day out of the week. I believe that all children should be given the opportunity to ride a train. We need to lobby in favor of more passenger trains to replace some cars especially in cities. This book is about a railroad line that never ran. I keep hoping that trains will soon return to the town I live in, Greenfield, Massachusetts.

You may contact me at   **New Email:**
                    Hampdenphil@gmail.com